FAIRNESS IN CRIMINAL JUSTICE

Golden Threads and Pragmatic Patches

British criminal justice is a principal legacy of Empire in the common law world. It attempts fairness between prosecutors and accused in an accusatory system for establishing criminal responsibility supervised by a judge who is conspicuously detached from the fray. Fundamental features, today recognised as human rights, include the presumption of innocence and onus of proof, the privilege against self-incrimination and the right to legal advice and representation. In these lectures, Dame Sian Elias examines modern challenges to this conception of criminal justice prompted by anxiety about crime and the costs and delays in proof of guilt. They include enlarged prosecutorial discretion in charging, incentivisation of early guilty pleas, adoption of reverse onuses of proof, application to criminal proceedings of principles of modern civil case management and measures to bring the victim into the criminal justice system. The lectures question whether this repositioning risks the integrity of the system.

DAME SIAN ELIAS has been Chief Justice of New Zealand since 1999. Educated in New Zealand and the United States, she has practised law since 1972. She was appointed a Queen's Counsel in 1988 and has held the position of Law Commissioner. She was appointed a High Court Judge in 1995 and was awarded the New Zealand Order of Merit in 1999. Dame Sian became a member of the New Zealand Supreme Court on its establishment in 2004.

FAIRNESS IN CRIMINAL JUSTICE

Golden Threads and Pragmatic Patches

DAME SIAN ELIAS

CAMBRIDGE
UNIVERSITY PRESS

CAMBRIDGE
UNIVERSITY PRESS

University Printing House, Cambridge CB2 8BS, United Kingdom

One Liberty Plaza, 20th Floor, New York, NY 10006, USA

477 Williamstown Road, Port Melbourne, VIC 3207, Australia

314–21, 3rd Floor, Plot 3, Splendor Forum, Jasola District Centre,
New Delhi – 110025, India

79 Anson Road, #06–04/06, Singapore 079906

Cambridge University Press is part of the University of Cambridge.

It furthers the University's mission by disseminating knowledge in the pursuit of
education, learning, and research at the highest international levels of excellence.

www.cambridge.org
Information on this title: www.cambridge.org/9781108474351
DOI: 10.1017/9781108625777

First published 2018

Printed and bound in Great Britain by Clays Ltd, Elcograf S.p.A.

A catalogue record for this publication is available from the British Library.

Library of Congress Cataloging-in-Publication Data
NAMES: Elias, Sian, author.
TITLE: Fairness in criminal justice : golden threads and pragmatic patches / Sian Elias.
DESCRIPTION: Cambridge, United Kingdom ; New York, NY : Cambridge University
Press, 2018. | Series: The Hamlyn lectures ; 2016. | Includes bibliographical references and
index.
IDENTIFIERS: LCCN 2018010829| ISBN 9781108474351 (alk. paper) | ISBN 9781108463157
(Paperback)
SUBJECTS: LCSH: Criminal justice, Administration of. | Justice. | University of Exeter.
School of Law. | LCGFT: Lectures.
CLASSIFICATION: LCC HV7419 .E49 2018 | DDC 172/.2–dc23
LC record available at https://lccn.loc.gov/2018010829

ISBN 978-1-108-47435-1 Hardback
ISBN 978-1-108-46315-7 Paperback

Cambridge University Press has no responsibility for the persistence or accuracy of URLs
for external or third-party internet websites referred to in this publication
and does not guarantee that any content on such websites is, or will remain,
accurate or appropriate.

CONTENTS

The Hamlyn Trust owes its existence today to the will of the late Miss Emma Warburton Hamlyn of Torquay, who died in 1941 at the age of eighty. She came of an old and well-known Devon family. Her father, William Bussell Hamlyn, practised in Torquay as a solicitor and Justice of the Peace for many years, and it seems likely that Miss Hamlyn founded the trust in his memory. Emma Hamlyn was a woman of strong character, intelligent and cultured, well-versed in literature, music and art, and a lover of her country. She travelled extensively in Europe and Egypt, and apparently took considerable interest in the law and ethnology of the countries and cultures that she visited. An account of Miss Hamlyn by Professor Chantal Stebbings of the University of Exeter may be found, under the title 'The Hamlyn Legacy', in volume 42 of the published Lectures.

Miss Hamlyn bequeathed the residue of her estate on trust in terms which it seems were her own. The wording was thought to be vague, and the will was taken to the Chancery Division of the High Court, which in November 1948 approved a Scheme for the administration of the trust. Paragraph 3 of the Scheme, which follows Miss Hamlyn's own wording, is as follows:

> The object of the charity is the furtherance by lectures or otherwise among the Common People of the United Kingdom of Great Britain and Northern Ireland of the

knowledge of the Comparative Jurisprudence and
Ethnology of the Chief European countries including the
United Kingdom, and the circumstances of the growth of
such jurisprudence to the Intent that the Common People
of the United Kingdom may realise the privileges which in
law and custom they enjoy in comparison with other
European Peoples and realising and appreciating such
privileges may recognise the responsibilities and
obligations attaching to them.

The Trustees are to include the vice-chancellor of the
University of Exeter; representatives of the Universities of
London, Glasgow, Belfast and Wales; and persons co-opted.
At present there are seven Trustees:

Ms Clare Dyer
Professor Rosa Greaves, University of Glasgow
Professor Roger Halson, University of Leeds
Professor John Morison, Queen's University, Belfast
The Rt Hon. Lord Justice Sedley
Professor Avrom Sherr, University of London
Professor Chantal Stebbings (representing the Vice-
    Chancellor of the University of Exeter) (Chair)

From the outset it was decided that the objects of the Trust
could be best achieved by means of an annual course of public
lectures of outstanding interest and quality by eminent lec-
turers, and by their subsequent publication and distribution
to a wider audience. The first of the Lectures were delivered by
the Rt Hon. Lord Justice Denning (as he then was) in 1949.
Since then there has been an unbroken series of annual
Lectures published until 2005 by Sweet & Maxwell, and

from 2006 by Cambridge University Press. A complete list of the Lectures may be found on pages ix to xiii. In 2005 the Trustees decided to supplement the Lectures with an annual Hamlyn Seminar, normally held at the Institute of Advanced Legal Studies in the University of London, to mark the publication of the Lectures in printed book form. The Trustees have also, from time to time, provided financial support for a variety of projects which, in various ways, have disseminated knowledge or have promoted to a wider public understanding of the law.

This, the 68th series of Lectures, was delivered by Dame Sian Elias, Chief Justice of New Zealand, at Cardiff University, the University of Exeter, and Lincoln's Inn Old Hall, London. The Board of Trustees would like to record its appreciation to Dame Sian and also the three institutions which so generously hosted these Lectures.

PROFESSOR CHANTAL STEBBINGS
Chair of the Trustees

The British model of criminal procedure and evidence is a principal legacy of Empire across the common law world. The practices and rules of proof applied in British criminal justice are likely to have been at the forefront of what Miss Hamlyn had in mind when she spoke of the privileges enjoyed by the common people of the United Kingdom, in comparison with other European peoples. At the ends of Empire, in New Zealand, they were privileges which were held up to Maori in 1840 as one of the benefits of the British citizenship obtained under the Treaty of Waitangi. It was understood that the system of state assumption of the responsibility of proving guilt in a process supervised by a judge who was conspicuously detached from the fray freed kin groups from burdens and risks that had become unsustainable. In these Lectures I attempt to pick up on Miss Hamlyn's wish to encourage recognition of 'the responsibilities and obligations' which attach to this inheritance.

Until comparatively recently the elements of criminal justice in common law jurisdictions were largely the work of judges in the exercise of what Lord Devlin in 1964 described as 'their power to see that what was fair and just was done between prosecutors and accused'. At about the same time in New Zealand a senior appellate judge, Sir Thaddeus McCarthy, felt able to say that keeping criminal practice and procedure fit for purpose 'ought always to be under the hands of the Judges'. Today criminal justice in all jurisdictions is increasingly the subject of enactments with far-reaching effect. The Criminal Procedure Rules 2005 in the United Kingdom have been described by Thomas LJ as having effected a 'sea change'. Similar transformation has been accomplished by reform in other common law jurisdictions.

The shift to enacted rules governing criminal procedure is only part of the picture. They have been accompanied by institutional and administrative restructuring (including of criminal legal aid, the delivery of prosecution and defence services, and court administration) which have changed the methods of delivery of criminal justice.

Changes include greater prosecutorial discretion in charging and diversion, measures to incentivise early guilty pleas, relaxation of unanimity in jury trials, reverse onuses of proof, restriction of the right to elect trial by jury, adoption of preventive orders and 'civil' penalties, application to criminal proceedings of modern civil case management measures, and efforts to bring the victim into the criminal justice system, in a 'triangulation' of the parties to whom fairness in procedure is owed. The effect has been a repositioning of criminal justice and the role of the judge in its administration. The procedural safeguards in criminal justice were developed to minimise error in proof of guilt and to meet wider rule of law values. In the Lectures I question whether they are being eroded in a way that undermines fundamental values in the legal order.

In the first Lecture I look at the elements of the criminal justice system as it stood when the first criminal trial was held in New Zealand in 1842 and as it has developed since. Those common to all British jurisdictions revolved around the roles of judge, jury, prosecutor, and defence counsel, and minimum standards of procedure such as the presumption of innocence and the privilege against self-incrimination. In the second Lecture I concentrate on the linked principles of the presumption of innocence and the right to silence and their application in the context of modern police methods designed to obtain confessions. In the final Lecture I look at the institutions through which criminal justice is delivered and the strains they face today.

The Lectures are published largely in the form in which they were delivered. I was privileged to deliver them at three outstanding institutions and with three distinguished chairmen, all of whom I count as dear friends. The first Lecture was given at the University of Cardiff, in acknowledgement of my Welsh heritage and with the Lord Chief Justice, Lord Thomas, as chairman. The second Lecture was given at the University of Exeter, in acknowledgement of Miss Hamlyn's own connec-tions, with Sir Stephen Sedley as chairman. The final Lecture was given at Lincoln's Inn, where I have the privilege of being an Honorary Bencher, with Lord Lester as chairman. I am grateful to the three institutions for their generous and warm hospitality and for providing me with knowledgeable and lively audiences. I express my thanks to those who chaired the Lectures smoothly and for their encouragement.

I am deeply grateful to Professor Chantal Stebbings, chair of the Hamlyn Trust, and to the Trustees for their confidence in me in this undertaking. I am conscious of the honour they have shown me and hope that they will think the project was worthwhile. I have greatly valued the generosity and company of the Trustees and am grateful for the spur they have provided to cause me to reflect on what matters in our system of criminal justice.

Lecture 1

'Fair and Just'?

My theme in these Lectures is 'criminal justice'.[1] I mean by that the practices and rules of proof and evidence applied by the courts in criminal cases. They were originally developed by judges in the exercise of what Lord Devlin described as 'their power to see that what was fair and just was done between prosecutors and accused' in a process that, he said, 'is still continuing'.[2] They aim to minimise error in the proof of guilt so that the innocent are not wrongly convicted. But they are also concerned to meet rule of law values which may not be fulfilled simply by formally correct proof.

Procedural law may seem unheroic, especially since my focus is on the proof of guilt in ordinary criminal cases. I am not going to talk about the extraordinary processes of closed hearings and special counsel which have exercised you in this country. So the topic may seem to be lawyers' law and dull stuff for a public lecture. I hope it does not appear so. It has been said that '[t]he history of liberty has largely been the history of observance of procedural

---

[1] It is the term suggested by William Twining to 'transcend any distinction between evidence and procedure' when considering the adjectival law observed by the courts in criminal trials: William Twining, 'What is the law of evidence?' in William Twining, *Rethinking Evidence: Exploratory Essays* (2nd edn, Cambridge University Press, 2006) 192 at 224.

[2] *Connelly* v. *Director of Public Prosecutions* [1964] AC 1254 (HL) at 1347–8.

safeguards'.[3] I like to think Miss Hamlyn would have agreed. The procedural safeguards of criminal justice may well have been one of the reasons for her confidence in the superiority of 'the privileges which in law and custom [the Common People of the United Kingdom] enjoy in comparison with other European Peoples'.

In looking at criminal justice today, I do not attempt demonstration of the superiority of the system we share by comparison with the criminal justice of other European Peoples. Rather, I want to look to Miss Hamlyn's further object in these Lectures in illuminating 'the responsibilities and obligations' which attach to the system we have inherited.

In recent years criminal justice has been the subject of close political attention and some public anxiety, reflecting wider policy debates and concern about law and order. None of that is likely to change fast. In a climate of anxiety about crime and the costs of the criminal justice system, maintaining the procedural safeguards necessary for the protection of liberty or legitimacy or rule of law values may not be seen as a priority. And it may not be popular. So I welcome the chance to talk about these matters in Lectures designed by Miss Hamlyn to be addressed to a wider audience than one of lawyers. How criminal justice is delivered tests commitment to the rule of law in any legal order.[4] In this Lecture I want to speak of the values that underlie the system of criminal justice

---

[3] *McNabb* v. *United States* 318 US 332 (1943) at 347 per Frankfurter J.

[4] It is why final courts of appeal have paid close attention to procedural law and evidence, as is described by the Hon. Michael Kirby in 'Why has the High Court become more involved in criminal appeals?' (2002) 23 *Aust Bar Rev* 4.

we share in the common law world and the institutional arrangements through which they are delivered. In the next two Lectures I talk about particular challenges they face today.[5]

A Recent Tradition

The system of criminal justice we observe is not ancient. The criminal trial and the law of procedure and evidence which has grown up around it were not found in a form which we would recognise until the nineteenth century. Criminal process before then has justly been described by Sir Stephen Sedley as 'a Hogarthian havoc of authoritarianism and anarchy'.[6]

Those charged were not presumed to be innocent. There was no disclosure of the prosecution evidence before trial. It was not until the beginning of the nineteenth century that all defendants were even entitled to a copy of the indictment.[7] Defendants were not entitled to legal

---

[5] In the second Lecture I concentrate on the presumption of innocence and the rights of silence (procedural values developed by the common law not only to promote correct decisions but also for rule of law and human rights reasons which have come to be reinforced with the adoption of human rights instruments). In the final Lecture I consider the institutional elements of the criminal justice system and the challenges they face today in keeping criminal justice fit for purpose.

[6] Stephen Sedley, 'Howzat?' (2003) 25(18), *London Review of Books* 15 at 16.

[7] Indictments were made available in trials for treason, or misprision of treason, under the Treason Act 1695 7 & 8 Will 3 c 3. In 1708 such prisoners also became entitled to a list of the witnesses and the jury: Treason Act 1708 7 Anne c 21, s 14. Stephens noted that provision of this information

representation, except in treason trials (and even then legal representation was a late development).[8] The law of evidence was so undeveloped that Edmund Burke denied that there was any such thing. The rules, he said, were so slight that 'a parrot he had known might get them by rote in one half-hour and repeat them in five minutes'.[9] James Fitzjames Stephen, in his monumental *History of the Criminal Law of England*, concluded that the evidence available from the *State Trials* series gave 'great reason to fear that the principles of evidence were then so ill understood, and the whole method of criminal procedure was so imperfect and superficial, that an amount of injustice frightful to think of must have been inflicted at the Assizes and Sessions on obscure persons of whom no one has ever heard or will hear'.[10] More recent scholarship, working from the Old Bailey records, amply supports Sir Stephen's deduction from the state trials about criminal process more generally.[11]

was seen as 'so great a favour that it ought to be reserved for people accused of a crime for which legislators themselves or their friends and connections were likely to be prosecuted' and that those legislators were 'comparatively indifferent as to the fate of people accused of sheep-stealing, or burglary, or murder': James Fitzjames Stephen, *A History of the Criminal Law of England* (MacMillan, London, 1883), vol. 1 at 225–6.

[8] Those charged with treason were allowed lawyers to represent them from 1695 under the Treason Act 1695 7 & 8 Will 3 c 3.

[9] *Lords' Journal*, 25 February 1794; cited in William Twining, 'The rationalist tradition of evidence scholarship' in William Twining, *Rethinking Evidence: Exploratory Essays* (2nd edn, Cambridge University Press, 2006) at 37.

[10] James Fitzjames Stephen, *A History of the Criminal Law of England* (MacMillan, London, 1883), vol. 1 at 402.

[11] J. H. Langbein, *Torture and the Law of Proof: Europe and England in the Ancien Régime* (University of Chicago Press, 1977). This research answers

The prohibition on legal representation was relaxed in the second half of the eighteenth century. It is estimated that by the end of that century one in three defendants appearing in the Old Bailey was represented by counsel.[12] A general right to legal representation was not, however, finally granted until 1836.[13] Before then, the complacent view was that the judge would represent the interests of the accused,[14] an assumption demonstrated time and again to be wrong.[15]

C. K. Allen's questioning of Stephen on this point on the basis that the ferocity and unfairness shown in the state trials may arise from the nature of such political offences in which acquittals would have been 'a direct and deadly blow at the Crown': C. K. Allen 'The presumption of innocence' in C. K. Allen, *Legal Duties and Other Essays in Jurisprudence* (Clarendon Press, Oxford, 1931) 253 at 261.

[12] J. M. Beattie, *Crime and the Courts in England, 1660–1800* (Clarendon Press, Oxford, 1986); cited by Stephen Sedley, 'Wringing out the fault: self-incrimination in the 21st century' (MacDermott Lecture, 2011), published in (2001) 52 *N Ir Legal Q* 107 at 112.

[13] Trials for Felony Act 1836 6 & 7 Will 4 ch. 114, s 1.

[14] Glanville Williams, *The Proof of Guilt* (The Hamlyn Lectures, Stevens & Sons, London, 1955) at 8–9. See also Stephen Sedley, 'Reading their rights' in Stephen Sedley, *Ashes and Sparks: Essays on Law and Justice* (Cambridge University Press, 2011) 29 at 35–6.

[15] An honourable exception was Chief Justice Holt. Of him, it was said that the prisoner whose spirit was 'broken with guilt' and was 'incapable of language to defend himself' could be confident that the judge would obtain from him all that was to his advantage and that he would 'wrest no law to destroy him nor conceal any that would save him': 'Life of Lord Chief Justice Holt' (1834) 11 Law Mag Quart Rev Juris 24 at 65. The comments are attributed to Sir Richard Steele with the note 'Where flattery could serve no purpose, contemporary eulogy has the best title to belief.'

Terrible injustice occurred because the procedures were so undeveloped. Men were condemned on the basis of hearsay evidence, much of it perjured or extracted from accomplices by torture or when they were under sentence of death and hoped to be reprieved.[16] Witnesses for the defence were not allowed to give sworn testimony and the jury was warned to treat their unsworn evidence with suspicion. Evidence of the bad character of the accused was freely given. Professor Milson says the 'miserable history of crime in England can be shortly told'.[17] 'Nothing worthwhile was created', he wrote. 'There is no achievement to trace. Except in so far as the maintenance of order is in itself admirable, nobody is to be admired before the age of reform.'

Following the political upheavals of the seventeenth century some principle started to emerge. In particular, it was accepted that the defendant was not to have his fault 'wrung out of him'.[18] It became established that out of court confessions were inadmissible at trial unless shown to have been 'voluntary'.[19] Since the defendant could not give sworn evidence at trial until the end of the nineteenth

---

[16] See Glanville Williams, *The Proof of Guilt* (The Hamlyn Lectures, Stevens & Sons, London, 1955) at 6; Stephen Sedley, 'Wringing out the fault: self-incrimination in the 21st century' (MacDermott Lecture, 2001) published in (2011) 52 *N Ir Legal Q* 107 at 110–17; J. H. Langbein, *Torture and the Law of Proof: Europe and England in the Ancien Régime* (University of Chicago Press, 1977).

[17] S. F. C. Milsom, *Historical Foundations of the Common Law* (Butterworths, London, 1969) at 353.

[18] William Blackstone, *Commentaries on the Laws of England* (S. Sweet, London, 1936) vol. 4 at 296.

[19] See *The King* v. *Rudd* (1775) 1 Leach 115 at 118; 168 ER 160 (KB) at 161.

century,[20] he could not be questioned at trial. The inability of the prosecution to question the defendant at trial was not, however, part of a more thoroughgoing right to silence.[21] The defendant's pre-trial interrogation, a process instituted in the sixteenth century,[22] was read out at trial. Pre-trial interrogation before Justices of the Peace was not preceded by a caution that the defendant was not obliged to answer questions until legislative reform in 1848.[23]

Before a defendant was allowed legal representation, the benefit of the immunity from being questioned at trial was effectively undermined. The defendant had to represent

[20] The defendant's right to give evidence was given in New Zealand in the Criminal Evidence Act 1889. It predated the equivalent reform in the English Criminal Evidence Act 1898 61 & 62 Vict c 36.

[21] The Phillips Royal Commission refers to an 1845 analytical digest which makes no mention of the right to silence: *Report of the Royal Commission on Criminal Procedure* (Cmnd 8092, January 1981) at 6. Procedures to protect individuals being investigated by the police were not developed until the Judges' Rules 1912, suggesting that the precept was not at the forefront of criminal justice.

[22] The practice was formalised by two statutes passed during the reign of King Philip and Queen Mary: 1 and 2 Phil & M c 13 (1554); and 2 & 3 Phil & M c 10 (1555). See also William Holdsworth, *A History of English Law* (Sweet & Maxwell, London, 1956) vol. 4 at 529–30.

[23] Administration of Justice (No 1) Act 1848 11 & 12 Vict c 42, s 18. The caution was to be in these terms: 'Having heard the Evidence, do you wish to say any thing in answer to the Charge? You are not obliged to say any thing unless you desire to do so, but whatever you say will be taken down in Writing, and may be given in Evidence against you upon your Trial.' Professor Glanville Williams observed that this was 'statutory compulsion' of a practice already followed by some magistrates: Glanville Williams, *The Proof of Guilt* (The Hamlyn Lectures, Stevens & Sons, London, 1955) at 43.

himself, and inevitably was drawn into providing his own, unsworn, account of the facts when challenging the witnesses against him. Until the right to counsel was secured, the participation of the defendant in conducting his own defence effectively prevented the development of the presumption of innocence or the modern burden of proof.[24]

The right to counsel transformed the dynamics of the criminal trial. The defendant no longer had to conduct his own defence and be drawn into giving his own account. The judge no longer had to pretend an obligation to look out for the interests of the defendant. The conditions were set up for development of the presumption of innocence and the responsibility of the prosecution to prove guilt. Criminal trial became an accusatorial proceeding focussed on the sufficiency of proof brought by the Crown.

The old pre-trial interrogation became a preliminary judicial hearing at which the defendant was cautioned that he was not obliged to say anything in response to the allegations but that anything he did say might be evidence against him. That paved the way for the pre-trial right to silence. Even so, it was not finally established until the abolition of the disqualification of the defendant from giving evidence at trial at the

---

[24] As recent examination of the records of trials at the Old Bailey shows, before the defendant was allowed representation, 'criminal procedure was essentially a dialogue between the accused, albeit unsworn, and the court': Stephen Sedley, 'Wringing out the fault: self-incrimination in the 21st century' (MacDermott Lecture, 2011), published in (2001) 52 *N Ir Legal Q* 107 at 111; discussing examples from J. H. Langbein, *Torture and the Law of Proof: Europe and England in the Ancien Régime* (University of Chicago Press, 1977) at 142.

end of the nineteenth century. Although now eligible to give evidence, the defendant had a right not to do so. No adverse comment on his failure to give evidence could be made by the prosecution.[25] Once the right not to give evidence was established, it came to be seen that it could not be undermined by pre-trial interrogation. These changes therefore established the conditions under which the presumption of innocence and the right to silence became foundations of modern criminal justice.[26]

The term 'right to silence' is used of a cluster of rights:[27] the right not to give evidence at trial, the privilege of a witness not to incriminate himself, and the right not to answer questions or give information in the pre-trial criminal investigation. These aspects of the right to silence arose at different times and without any overarching design.[28] Wigmore says the policy underpinning the privilege is

---

[25] Criminal Evidence Act 1898 61 & 62 Vict c 36, s 2(b).

[26] The right to silence is not a feature of British criminal justice only. Characterisation of other European systems as ones that require defendants to speak in their own defence is quite wrong: see for example Glanville Williams, *The Proof of Guilt* (The Hamlyn Lectures, Stevens & Sons, London, 1955) at 60.

[27] Lord Mustill said of the right to silence: 'In truth it does not denote any single right, but rather refers to a disparate group of immunities, which differ in nature, origin, incidence and importance': *R* v. *Director of Serious Fraud Office, ex p Smith* [1993] AC 1 (HL) at 30.

[28] H. E. Smith, 'The modern privilege: its nineteenth-century origins' in R. H. Helmholz (ed) *The Privilege Against Self-Incrimination: Its Origins and Development* (Chicago University Press, 1997) 145 at 156; J. H. Langbein, 'The historical origins of the privilege against self-incrimination at common law' (1994) 92 *Mich L Rev* 1047; Pat McInerney, 'The privilege against self-incrimination from early origins to Judges' Rules: challenging the "orthodox view"' (2014) 18(2) *E & P* 101 at 109.

'anything but clear'.[29] That is not to say, however, that there is not principled justification to be made. Laskin J, in the Supreme Court of Canada, grounded the right to silence in the presumption of innocence. He thought that the presumption of innocence 'in a more refined sense' gave the accused both 'the initial benefit of a right of silence' and the 'ultimate benefit' of any reasonable doubt.[30] With slightly different emphasis, another Canadian judge, Lamer CJ, thought that the Crown's 'burden of establishing guilt' together with 'the right of silence' were the essential elements of the presumption of innocence.[31] He described the 'right of silence' as 'the concept of a "case to meet"'. He took the view that the presumption of innocence and the initial benefit of the right to silence themselves were behind the 'non-compellability right', the right not to give evidence.

Whatever their historical origins, the presumption of innocence and the right to silence are now established as human rights in modern charters of rights. So too is the wider and absolute right to fair trial.[32] The human right to fair trial extends beyond fulfilment of the process rights in

---

[29] John Henry Wigmore, *Evidence in Trials at Common Law* (McNaughton rev. edn, Aspen Law and Business, United States, 1961), vol. 8 at 318.

[30] *R v. Appleby* [1972] SCR 303 at 317.

[31] *Dubois v. The Queen* [1985] 2 SCR 350 at 357–8.

[32] *Brown v. Stott* [2003] 1 AC 681 (PC) at 784 per Lord Bingham and at 708 per Lord Steyn. Lord Hope considered that the constituent rights in the European Convention are themselves absolute (such as the right to representation in Art. 6(3)) although implied rights (such as the privilege against self-incrimination) are not: at 719.

court.[33] Chief Justice Mason of the High Court of Australia, in affirming a broad inherent discretion to prevent the processes of the court being used unfairly, grounded the power in a right to fair trial which embraced the 'whole course of the criminal process':[34]

> [The right to fair trial] is one of several entrenched in our legal system in the interests of seeking to ensure that innocent people are not convicted of criminal offences. As such, it is more commonly manifested in rules of law and of practice designed to regulate the course of the trial: see *Bunning* v. *Cross*;[35] *Reg* v. *Sang*.[36] But there is no reason why the right should not extend to the whole course of the criminal process and it is inconceivable that a trial which could not fairly proceed should be compelled to take place on the grounds that such a course did not constitute an abuse of process.

The principles and rules of criminal justice were for the most part settled by judges, as Lord Devlin said in 1964, according to ideas of what is fair and just and what is best calculated to deliver verdicts that are safe.[37] In 1969, a judge of the New Zealand Court of Appeal felt able to say that practice and procedure 'ought always to be under the hands of the Judges' so that they can clear away rules that are 'no longer helpful but [have become]

---

[33] *Jago* v. *District Court of New South Wales* (1989) 168 CLR 23; *Salduz* v. *Turkey* (2008) 49 EHRR 421 (ECHR).

[34] *Jago* v. *District Court of New South Wales* (1989) 168 CLR 23 at 29.

[35] *Bunning* v. *Cross* (1978) 141 CLR 54.   [36] *R* v. *Sang* [1980] AC 402 (HL).

[37] *Connelly* v. *Director of Public Prosecutions* [1964] AC 1254 (HL) at 1347–8.

obstructive'.[38] Today that responsibility is increasingly undertaken by Parliament and the executive. There are benefits in terms of accessibility and democratic legitimacy in enacted rules, but there are other consequences too.

There may be less scope for judges to adapt rules and practices to meet changing needs thrown up in actual cases.[39] Some enactments capture pre-existing common law rules of evidence and procedure and may not be intended to inhibit its further development. But some reform is more thoroughgoing and affects common law development of criminal justice.[40]

In their application, the principles and values of criminal justice turn increasingly on how texts are interpreted. That has implications for judicial method in particular cases.[41] It also affects cross-jurisdictional comparisons and

---

[38] McCarthy J in *Smith* v. *Police* [1969] NZLR 856 (SC) at 860; and *Jorgensen* v. *News Media (Auckland) Ltd* [1969] NZLR 961 (CA) at 994.

[39] The common law, as Benjamin Cardozo, Lord Goff, and others have pointed out is a method of change: see Benjamin Cardozo, *The Growth of the Law* (Yale University Press, New Haven, 1924) at 73; and Lord Goff, 'The Wilberforce Lecture: the future of the common law' (1997) 46 *Intl & Comp LQ* 745 at 754.

[40] Section 202 of New Zealand's Evidence Act 2006 provides for periodic review of the Act's operation by the Law Commission. The most recent review led Parliament to enact legislation amending several of the Act's provisions. The continued involvement of Parliament, combined with the Act's fairly limited references to the continuing relevance of common law rules of evidence, means there is some uncertainty about the scope the Act leaves for judicial development.

[41] As is illustrated by the reasoning of the New Zealand Supreme Court in *R* v. *Wichman* [2015] NZSC 198, [2016] 1 NZLR 753: see in particular the text accompanying Lecture 2, n. 226 below.

borrowings, since care must be taken with variations in legislative text and policies.[42] There has always been variation between common law jurisdictions. Over time, however, differences tended to subside because the ends of criminal justice grow from a common root and have been relatively constant. They have turned on general insights from logic and experience in matters of proof and values of the wider legal order such as equal and fair treatment which are part of the rule of law. More caution is now required in looking to the decisions of other jurisdictions because they increasingly reflect statutory provisions and policies which may differ and point to different outcomes even where common problems arise.

In addition, the shift away from judicial responsibility for procedure and evidence occurs in a climate of politicisation of substantive criminal law which is a feature of our times. The move from judicial responsibility for the procedural law of criminal justice in part may reflect dissatisfaction with its costs and outcomes. Judges may no longer be trusted to have criminal justice 'under [their] hands'. And it may no longer seem an adequate explanation of the ends of criminal justice that it seeks to achieve 'that what was fair and just was done between prosecutors and accused', as Lord Devlin thought was its object. In a number of jurisdictions today enacted rules prescribing the practice of the courts are concerned not only with these matters but with more instrumental ends such as efficiency, cost-effectiveness, and meeting the interests of victims.

---

[42] A matter illustrated by the covert policing cases I discuss in the second Lecture.

A New Country

In New Zealand, we like to think of ourselves as 'a new country with little history'.[43] This sort of 'parrot-cry' profoundly irritated our most distinguished historian, John Beaglehole. He urged us to regard ourselves as being as 'old as civilisation'.[44] Because 'civilisation' in criminal law was only just emerging in England when New Zealand was ceded to the British Crown in 1840, we did not have much to inherit. Indeed, in some respects local circumstances meant that some reforms of criminal justice later adopted in England were established first in New Zealand and other British overseas possessions. In England in 1840 the prosecution of crime was still largely undertaken by the private individuals affected. Although the setting up of the police force from 1820 was beginning to transform prosecution, it was not until 1880 that a Crown Prosecution Service was established.[45] In New Zealand, the prosecution of crime was always undertaken by public prosecutors.[46]

---

[43] As Sir Edmund Hillary, visiting Europe for the first time, described it. Edmund Hillary, *View from the Summit* (Doubleday, London, 1999) at 65.

[44] J. C. Beaglehole, 'The New Zealand scholar' in Peter Munz (ed.) *The Feel of Truth: Essays in New Zealand and Pacific History* (A. H. and A. W. Reed, Wellington, 1969) 237 at 244.

[45] Under the Prosecution of Offences Act 1879 42 & 43 Vict c 22.

[46] In New Zealand from 1840 the prosecution of crime was shared by the police and by the Attorney-General. In 1864 they were reorganised through Crown solicitors and the police in each centre, in an arrangement that continues today. The regulations under which these arrangements were put in place recited that they were made 'having regard to the difference of circumstances between England and New

At the signing of the Treaty of Waitangi, there had been much talk about the benefits to be obtained from English law. There was urgent need to bring the lawless elements of the European population under control. And Maori themselves were exhausted by the wars and blood feuds which were the result of collective responsibility of kin-groups in pre-European society and which had been taken to a new level since the arrival of muskets. Whole populations had been uprooted from their tribal lands, causing disputes about land that still vex our legal system today. With that background, it is not surprising that 'the coming of the law' was said to have been 'hailed by Maori as enthusiastically as the coming of the gospel'.[47]

The first substantial test for the new legal order after the Treaty of Waitangi was the trial for murder of a 16-year-old Maori named Maketu Wharetotara.[48] Maketu was accused of killing five people on what is an idyllic island in the Bay of Islands that still bears the name of the family who farmed it and whose members were among those killed.[49]

Zealand': 'Criminal prosecutions' (3 March 1864) 8 *New Zealand Gazette* 86.

[47] Alan Ward, *A Show of Justice: Racial 'Amalgamation' in Nineteenth Century New Zealand* (Auckland University Press, 1974) at 136.

[48] Maketu was baptised as Wiremu Kingi shortly prior to his execution: see Stephen Oliver, 'Maketu, Wiremu Kingi' from the *Dictionary of New Zealand Biography* (30 October 2012) Te Ara Encyclopedia of New Zealand, available at: www.teara.govt.nz (last accessed 6 October 2016).

[49] John and Elizabeth Roberton bought the island of Motuarohia (also known as 'Roberton's Island') from local Maori for £213 in 1839, and built a farmhouse using 'nearby boulders' as a foundation. John Roberton drowned while sailing in 1840. See Paul Moon, 'Maketu's execution and

Maketu worked for the widow who owned the property, Mrs Roberton. As the son of a chief, he seems to have resented the way he was treated by the farm manager. The Crown case was that he had killed the manager and then despatched Mrs Roberton and her two children, together with a foster child who was half-Maori.

The trial was less than two years after the signing of the Treaty. There was some doubt about how the Maori population, which greatly outnumbered the European population at the time, would react to the assertion of criminal jurisdiction over one of their own. Although Maketu was eventually delivered into the custody of the police magistrate, there was considerable agitation among Maori in the Bay of Islands and the Europeans living there feared violence. The matter was more complicated, however, than a crime by Maori against Europeans. The half-Maori child who was one of the victims was the granddaughter of a principal chief in the Bay of Islands.[50]

In the end, some twenty Northland chiefs, including Maketu's father, wrote to the Governor to disassociate themselves from his actions and to make it clear they left him to be

---

the extension of British sovereignty in New Zealand' (2013) 6(1) *Te Kaharoa* 36 at 37.

[50] Prominent missionary Henry Williams considered that 'had not the grandchild of Rewa been one of the victims, thus bringing all the Ngapuhi tribes as auxiliaries to the Europeans in the event of war', Maketu would not have been given up by his tribe without a fight: Letter from Henry Williams to James Busby (British Resident) (20 April 1842); quoted in Paul Moon, 'Maketu's execution and the extension of British sovereignty in New Zealand' (2013) 6(1) *Te Kaharoa* 36 at 43–4.

dealt with according to British law.[51] It seems that these chiefs were concerned that retribution against Maketu's tribe would be exacted, either by Europeans or by other tribes related to the murdered Maori child. There was fear that wider tribal groups would be drawn into war. In their letter, the chiefs asked that Maketu not be returned to the Bay of Islands and emphasised that he had acted alone and was responsible alone.

[51] The letter read: 'Governor We, the Ngapuhi, have assembled at Paihia to consider the reports that have flown about in the wind. The reports are many, and are now caught. Governor, we are quite downcast with the work of the tongue. Now, the work of Maketu lies quite plain. That deed was his alone, although the Europeans are jealous, supposing that we, the natives, have a heart for mischief. No, no Governor, we have no mischievous intentions towards the Europeans; it is all regard. It is true formerly we had a heart; now we have not our old hearts for slaughter and murder. No, Governor, here are the resolutions of our Assembly forwarded to you, that you may fully see the greatness of our hearts for mischief or not. Sir, Maketu's work is his alone, his own; we have nothing to say for him. That man is with you; leave him there. Do not bring him back here to us; lest there be a disturbance, leave him there. Governor, do not listen to the reports that have flown about in the wind . . . Sir, Governor, let your regard be great for us, the children of the Queen Victoria, the Queen of England, of Europe also. Now, this is the word of the book: "Love one another." This is a good word. Shew us the greatness of your regard to us and our children, and we shall all turn without one exception to Victoria to be her children. But if not, what shall we do? Governor, here we are sitting in ignorance; we have no thoughts; you are our parent. Do you write a book to us, a book to raise us up, who are sitting in darkness, in the woods or elsewhere. We have no mischievous dispositions towards the Europeans. No, no. "Love one another".' See: Paul Moon, 'Maketu's execution and the extension of British sovereignty in New Zealand' (2013) 6(1) *Te Kaharoa* 36 at 45; see also *R* v. *Maketu* SC Auckland, 1 March 1842 at 2–3, available at: www.victoria.ac.nz/law/nzl ostcases/.

Maketu's trial took place in the first criminal sittings of the Supreme Court held after the arrival in New Zealand of the first Chief Justice, William Martin. Martin took care to use the opportunity to demonstrate the superiority of British justice both in punishing only the perpetrator responsible, rather than his tribe, and also in the careful method of public proof before a judge and jury. It helped the Chief Justice's purpose in demonstrating British justice that at the same sitting of the court there was the trial of a European for criminal assault on a Maori. The defendant, well-known and apparently respectable, was convicted and sentenced to two years' hard labour, showing the impartiality and inexorability of the law.

The courtroom was packed for both trials. The proceedings were translated into Maori. The newspapers, English and Maori, carried extensive coverage of Maketu's trial. They are the only contemporary record of what took place. Since the reports are incomplete and do not entirely coincide, what we know of the trial is sketchy and some of the details obtained from a single source may not be entirely accurate, particularly in the translation of the terms used.

The trial was before the Chief Justice and a jury of twelve Europeans. The prosecutor was William Swainson, the Attorney-General. Maketu was represented by C. B. Brewer. The procedure was fully explained to the public gallery by the judge, starting with the selection of the jury and the challenges available to the defence. Brewer immediately challenged the jurisdiction of the Court to try Maketu on the grounds that he could not know 'the requirements of the laws of England'.[52] He also objected to the composition of the jury and asked for a jury of equal numbers of Maori and Pakeha. The Crown opposed the applications on the basis that the Treaty of Waitangi had provided one law for Maori and Pakeha (Europeans) alike.[53] The Chief Justice ruled in favour of the Crown on the jurisdiction point. He also dismissed the application for a mixed jury on the basis that Maketu was a British subject and was not entitled to be tried otherwise than by an ordinary jury.[54]

In an account written some years later, Swainson described the impression produced on those packed into the courtroom to watch the case. He remarked on the deep effect of the 'quiet calmness with which the inquiry was conducted; the patient painstaking care of the Chief Justice; the grave

[52] See 'Ko Te Wakwakanga O Maketu', *Te Karere o Nui Tireni* (Auckland, 1 April 1842) at 13–17. The translation is from *R v. Maketu* SC Auckland, 1 March 1842, available at: www.victoria.ac.nz/law/nzlostcases/ (last accessed 6 October 2016) at page 9.

[53] The newspaper report, written in Maori, has been translated into English as having the Crown prosecutor say: 'Yes, it is right that he be judged, as the Queen's book [the Treaty of Waitangi] has been widely discussed, which says, that there should be one rule for all people of this land, whether Maori or Pakeha [European].' In agreeing with the Crown submission, the Chief Justice is reported as saying that it was 'right for him to be judged'.

[54] The property qualification for jurors which applied under the Juries Ordinance 1841 5 Vict 3 in effect disqualified Maori, whose lands were held communally. It was not until an 1844 Ordinance that the property qualification was removed for the purposes of constituting mixed juries where the case affected the person or property of 'any aboriginal native of New Zealand': Juries Amendment Ordinance 1844 7 Vict 2, s 1.

attention of the jury; [and] the solemn stillness of the awful moment which immediately preceded [the verdict]'.[55] Similar effect was produced at the sentence hearing two days later, when Maketu was condemned to death. The Chief Justice himself wrote later of the trial that the 'spectacle of our criminal trials' produced a great effect on the witnesses and those who heard the story as it was 'carried throughout the land':[56]

> Tardy they thought our procedure to be, and even cruel;
> but men accustomed to the indiscriminate vengeance of
> tribe against tribe were struck with awe at the sight of
> a system, which slowly yet surely, tracked out the single
> shedder of blood, and smote him alone. The execution of
> Maketu was approved everywhere; even in the north
> among his own people, it was not resented.

Although Martin and Swainson were satisfied with the trial and the impression it produced, the newspaper reports of the trial show that our perceptions of fairness in trial process have developed since 1842. Maketu had not originally been a suspect. The only evidence against him was his admissions.

The first was made to a European shopkeeper, Thomas Spicer. Spicer acknowledged when cross-examined that he was not fluent in Maori and that Maketu spoke no English. He said that Maketu had been pointed out to him as the murderer. He said he had then confronted Maketu 'several

---

[55] W. Swainson, *New Zealand and its Colonisation* (Smith Elder, London, 1859) at 58–9.

[56] William Martin, 'Observations on the proposal to take native lands under an act of the assembly' [1864] I *AJHR* E2c at 6.

times in the course of the day' to attempt to get him to admit what had happened. He was unsuccessful for much of the day. Spicer's evidence was that eventually, however, Maketu admitted his responsibility. One newspaper report quoted Spicer's evidence as being that he had 'continued to chastise [Maketu] and then he finally admitted it'.[57] Spicer could not remember what he had said to Maketu to cause him to confess but the newspaper reports of what he said at the trial suggest that he was proud of being the one who had obtained the confession.

There was evidence that Maketu had also acknowledged his responsibility at the inquest into the deaths. This evidence was objected to by Brewer on the grounds that Maketu had not been cautioned by the coroner before being questioned, as the law required. The interpreter at the inquest[58] gave evidence that he had told Maketu he was 'not compelled to speak without he liked', but does not seem to have recalled any caution by the coroner.[59] Fortunately for the Crown, the ubiquitous Mr Spicer had been on the inquest jury. He said that he had heard the

---

[57] This account is taken from the Maori language paper, *Te Karere o Nui Tireni*, and has been translated into English (see above at n. 52). Since Spicer's evidence was given in English and translated into Maori and the Maori language report is cited in its further translation into English, it is not possible to be confident about the use of the word 'chastise'. Spicer's meaning does not seem to have been explored at trial or, if it was, no report of the examination has come down to us.

[58] George Clarke Junior, who held office as a 'Protector of Aborigines' within the colonial government.

[59] Although if one had been given it must have been translated by him into Maori, since Maketu did not speak English.

21

caution given. The judge allowed the evidence of the admission at the inquest.

In his address to the jury, Brewer explained that he had been retained only that morning, 'about an hour before the trial came on'. There had been no opportunity for him to communicate with Maketu, nor had he seen the depositions before coming into court. Even though the judge had dismissed the objection to jurisdiction, Brewer urged the jury to place weight upon the fact that Maketu was ignorant of the laws under which he was prosecuted and had 'no possible means or opportunity of understanding them'. Not knowing the consequences of confessing, it was possible he had not told the truth and could have made the statement in order to shield others. Brewer also suggested that Spicer's evidence as to the first confession was not entitled to 'much credit' both because he did not perfectly understand the Maori language and because, as Brewer said, 'to say the least, Mr Spicer was rather too importunate in obtaining [the admissions]'. Brewer pointed out that the second confession simply followed on from the first and that there were similar concerns about Maketu's capacity to understand what he was being asked. Brewer ended his address by referring to the lack of other evidence against Maketu and to the presumption of innocence: 'Where there is any doubt as to the guilt of a prisoner, the humanity of the law of England always directs that the benefit of such doubt should be given in favour of the prisoner.' The jury was apparently not troubled by doubt. The newspaper reports indicate that the verdict of guilty was returned after a retirement of a few minutes only.

A number of observations about the characteristics of British criminal justice may be made from this first New Zealand trial. They raise themes I explore in these Lectures. In the trial can be seen the elements of criminal process we still observe today, both institutional arrangements and the emerging values and principles which are applied.

Judge & Co

Maketu's trial revolved around the roles of judge, jury, prosecutor, and defence counsel in a public and formal hearing. The sufficiency of proof of guilt was then assessed, as it is in modern jury trials, by the trier of fact, in his case a lay jury of twelve.[60] The verdict was arrived at on the basis of evidence laid out at trial by a prosecutor representing the state. The evidence was tested by a lawyer representing the accused

---

[60] A jury comprises twelve persons in New Zealand, in Crown Court and High Court criminal proceedings in England and Wales, in Canada and in Australia. In some jurisdictions (e.g. Canada and Western Australia), more than twelve jurors can be sworn at the start of the trial but only twelve can deliberate. In Scotland, trials have fifteen jurors. Majority verdicts are allowed (with some conditions) in New Zealand (Juries Act 1981, s 29C), England and Wales (Juries Act 1974, s 17), Scotland (Criminal Procedure Act 1995, s 90 – which allows for majorities as low as 8/15) and almost all of the Australian jurisdictions (Jury Act 1995 (Q), s 59A; Juries Act 1927 (SA), s 57; Juries Act 2000 (Vic), s 46; Jury Act 1977 (NSW), s 55F). Majority verdicts are not permitted in Canada (Criminal Code RSC 1985 c C-46, s 653(1)) or in the Australian Commonwealth jurisdiction (Commonwealth Constitution, s 80 and *Cheatle* v. *The Queen* (1993) 177 CLR 541). Likewise, the Western Australian and ACT statutes (Juries Act 1957 (WA) and Juries Act 1967 (ACT)) make no provision for majority verdicts in criminal trials.

(who could have called, but in Maketu's case did not call, evidence for the defence). The whole was supervised by a judge who was detached from the fray and directed the jury, not as to its verdict, but as to the law. The detachment of the judge is perhaps the most striking feature of our system by comparison with the features of other systems. I suspect, however, that most people would say that it is the role of the jury that sets our system apart.

Sir Alfred Denning, in the first Hamlyn Lectures, had no doubt about the importance of the jury as a protector of freedom.[61] 'Time and time again', he said, 'the jury has been found to be our safeguard.' Others have been more sceptical. Professor Glanville Williams considered that judicial approval of retention of jury trial 'may sometimes mean that the jury does no harm, which is not to say that it is of any positive use'.[62] He was inclined to think that the jury did 'little harm' because the judge, in summing up on the facts, was able to give the jury a steer which was followed 'sufficiently often to give an appearance of reliability to the mode of trial'.[63] As Williams acknowledged, his lukewarm praise was hardly 'any strong argument for a continuation of the system'.[64]

---

[61] Alfred Denning, *Freedom Under The Law* (The Hamlyn Lectures, Stevens & Sons, London, 1949) at 55.

[62] Glanville Williams, *The Proof of Guilt* (The Hamlyn Lectures, Stevens & Sons, London, 1955) at 224.

[63] *Ibid.* at 241.

[64] A disadvantage of the jury system was thought by Williams to be the difficulties of overturning a jury verdict on appeal because of the 'exaggerated deference accorded to [it]': at 259–61. It was 'far easier for a person convicted by a jury to win an appeal on an unmeritorious point of procedure or evidence than to re-open on appeal the really serious

It is true that the option of trial by judge alone is increasingly taken by defendants where it is available and that jury trials are discouraged or limited to more serious offending by legislation in many common law jurisdictions. But there is rather more to be said for the institution of the jury than that it does 'little harm'. The participation of members of the community in the determination of guilt in serious cases is an important civic responsibility we would lose if trials were undertaken by professional judges only. The involvement of jurors aids in wider public understanding of the legal system and dispels the complacency that comes with habit and repetition. Many of the standards applied in criminal law turn on values the jury is well placed to apply.[65] The jury provides legitimacy for the criminal justice system which we should, I think, be reluctant to disturb.[66]

Maketu was prosecuted by the Attorney-General for the Crown. The importance of the shift from private to public prosecution in the name of the state should not be underestimated. 'Crime is crime', as Sir Carleton Allen once remarked, 'because it is wrongdoing which directly and in serious degree threatens the security or well-being of

question of his guilt'. I tend to agree that the reluctance to supervise the verdict on appeal is a problem in the system of criminal justice, but think it reflects more on our appellate system (a topic I consider further in my third Lecture, below at the text accompanying Lecture 3, n. 385).

[65] That does not mean to say that juror 'leniency' is something for which our system allows latitude, as is sometimes suggested: see *B (SC12/2013) v. R* [2013] NZSC 151, [2014] 1 NZLR 261 at [28] per Elias CJ.

[66] That is particularly so in a jurisdiction like New Zealand where other lay participation in the criminal justice system is extremely limited, by comparison with the extensive lay magistracy of England and Wales.

society.'[67] Allen's view was that it was not safe to leave crime to private redress. He thought crime must be controlled by a public authority 'more powerful and less erratic than the private plaintiff'. Crown prosecution also underscores the public law values and interests served by the prosecution of crime and positions criminal justice within the wider constitutional frame.

The defendant's right to be represented by a lawyer, now recognised as an aspect of the human right of fair trial, does not itself ensure representation. Not all defendants want to be legally represented. Many cannot afford legal representation or think the cost is not worth incurring. And current debates about the extent to which legal representation should be provided at public expense indicate that there is a range of legitimate views about the extent to which lawyers should be provided to those who cannot obtain them. No one who has seen an unrepresented defendant in a serious criminal case can, however, be under any illusion about the disadvantage. It is why courts from time to time stay cases until legal representation is provided for those without the means to pay,[68] or overturn on judicial review as unreasonable

---

[67] C. K. Allen, 'The nature of a crime' (1931) *J Comp Legis & Intl Law* (3rd series) 1 at 11.

[68] *Dietrich* v. *R* (1992) 177 CLR 293; *Powell* v. *Alabama* 287 US 45 (1932) at 68–9; *Giddeon* v. *Wainright* 372 US 335 (1963) at 343–5. In *Dietrich*, Brennan J dissented on the ground that the decision was an unwarranted intrusion into legislative and executive functions. Dawson J dissented on the basis that the law recognised no right for an accused to be represented at public expense, and that the interests of justice cannot be 'pursued without regard to other considerations' that the courts were not well-placed to assess (at 349–50).

decisions of legal aid authorities declining legal aid,[69] or set aside convictions where lack of legal representation has meant that the trial has been unfair.[70] It is why the right to have legal assistance provided if the defendant does not have the means to pay for it is in many jurisdictions recognised as a human right.[71]

The detachment of the judge may be more obvious when a jury is the finder of fact, but what really enables detachment is the separate and independent functions performed by prosecutor and defence counsel. The judge is relieved of the need to investigate the proof or the need to look out for the interests of an unrepresented defendant or the interests of the community in prosecution. He is released to be a neutral umpire. The habit of detachment of the judge,[72]

---

[69] *Marteley* v. *The Legal Services Commissioner* [2015] NZSC 127, [2016] 1 NZLR 633.

[70] *R* v. *Condon* [2006] NZSC 62, [2007] 1 NZLR 300; *McInnis* v. *The Queen* (1979) 143 CLR 575 at 579–80; *R* v. *Kirk* (1982) 76 Cr App R 194 (CA); *R* v. *Harris* [1985] Crim LR 244 (CA); see also *R* v. *Taito* [2001] UKPC 50, [2001] UKPC 59, [2003] 3 NZLR 577. Under s 30 of the Sentencing Act 2002 (NZ), no person can be imprisoned unless given the opportunity to have legal representation at the point at which he or she was at risk of conviction. If a sentence of imprisonment is imposed, the conviction (not just the sentence) can be quashed on appeal.

[71] International Covenant on Civil and Political Rights, Art. 14(3)(d); European Convention on Human Rights, Art. 6(3)(c); New Zealand Bill of Rights Act 1990, s 24(f); Human Rights Act 2004 (ACT), s 22(2)(f); Charter of Human Rights and Responsibilities Act 2006 (Vic), s 25(2)(f).

[72] Pollock and Maitland suggested that: 'The judges sit in court, not in order that they may discover the truth, but in order that they may answer the question, "How's that?"' and that 'This passive habit seems to grow upon them as time goes on': Frederick Pollock and Frederic Maitland,

the characteristic of common law method, is carried over into trials where the judge determines fact without a jury. The prosecutor and defence counsel fulfil the same roles in a judge-alone trial as in a jury trial. The judge comes to the case only as a judge, to determine whether the proof offered by the prosecutor and tested by the defence is sufficient if the judge is the trier of fact or to ensure that the evidence is properly admissible for consideration by the jury. The general bases for excluding evidence as inadmissible are that it is insufficiently probative (that is to say helpful in proving a fact), that it was improperly obtained, and that its admission would be unfair.

The final feature of British criminal justice demonstrated in Maketu's case was its conduct in public. The proof of guilt was then, as now, an open and formal process. The institutional elements of independent prosecutor acting for the state rather than for any individual, defence counsel acting for the defendant, and the judge as umpire or impartial decision-maker in a formal public hearing set up the conditions for the accusatory system of trial. As I have discussed, the division of responsibilities allowed development of the rules of evidence and proof and the process values observed in criminal justice.

The impression of deliberation and dispassionate and disinterested examination of proof which used to impress the Maori observers of Maketu's trial (and to persuade them of the benefits of British legal process) are virtues

The History of English Law Before the Time of Edward I (2nd edn, Cambridge University Press, 1898) at 671.

of the system. They were recent developments in British justice at the time of Maketu's trial, although glimpses of the ideas on which they were based can be seen much earlier. Cool dispassionate delivery of criminal justice may not, however, have featured much before the period. It became possible only when the prosecution of crime was seen as a function of the state, not the private citizens who were directly affected, and when the judge was freed to be disinterested in relation to prosecution and defence. The challenges facing these elements today represent a topic I return to in the third Lecture.

Golden Threads in Criminal Justice

Sir Stephen Sedley may be right that 'presumed innocence, strict proof, and ... silent defendants made the nineteenth century a criminal lawyer's heyday'.[73] And there are many who think that things have only got worse. There is a widespread view that modern criminal justice 'puts blinders over the eyes of the trier of fact'[74] in favour of the guilty. In an age of popular anxiety about crime, such views resonate with the public and with legislators. They are views that were best

---

[73] Stephen Sedley, 'Wringing out the fault: self-incrimination in the 21st century' (MacDermott Lecture, 2001) published in (2011) 52 *N Ir Legal Q* 107 at 118; although, as Sedley says elsewhere, there is 'nothing to be said, even comparatively' for the system of criminal justice it replaced: Stephen Sedley, 'Howzat?' (2003) 25(18), *London Review of Books* 15.

[74] *R v. Corbett* [1988] 1 SCR 670 at 691 per Dickson CJ. He took the view that such blinders should be avoided except as a last resort. In most cases the jury should be given all relevant information and the matter could be left to its good sense, with appropriate 'clear instructions in law from the trial judge regarding the extent of its probative value'.

pressed by Jeremy Bentham at about the time that modern criminal justice was taking off. His sparkling dismissals of the various scruples against requiring a defendant to contribute to the search for truth as the 'foxhunter's reason' or the 'old woman's reason' continue to buffet the law of criminal justice today.[75] It is I think time to move on. The arguments are not

[75] Jeremy Bentham, *Rationale of Judicial Evidence* (J. S. Mill, ed., Hunt and Clarke, London, 1827) at 230–8. In *Palko* v. *Connecticut* 302 US 319 (1937) at 325–6 Cardozo J said that the 'immunity from compulsory self-incrimination' was not 'of the very essence of a scheme of ordered liberty', noting that 'today as in the past there are students of our penal system who look upon the immunity as a mischief rather than a benefit' (in reference to Bentham) and argued that 'Justice . . . would not perish if the accused were subject to a duty to respond to orderly inquiry'. It is certainly correct that a miscarriage of justice arises also from acquittal of the guilty, as Viscount Simon LC said in *Stirland* v. *DPP* [1944] AC 315 (HL) at 324. And C. K. Allen agrees with Bentham that if too many guilty persons are set free in order to safeguard the innocent there will come a point where 'the whole system of justice has broken down': C. K. Allen, 'The presumption of innocence' in C. K. Allen, *Legal Duties and Other Essays in Jurisprudence* (Clarendon Press, Oxford, 1931) 253 at 287. Williams expresses the view that acquittal of the guilty may put strain on the whole system of justice – it may lead to the police disregarding limits and to public demand for more severe punishment: Glanville Williams, *The Proof of Guilt* (The Hamlyn Lectures, Stevens & Sons, London, 1955) at 133. Some commentators suggest that police trickery, of the kind I discuss in the second Lecture (see below at the text accompanying Lecture 2, n. 230 and following), arises out of this sort of frustration: Kingsley Hyland and Clive Walker, 'Undercover policing and underwhelming laws' [2014] *Crim LR* 555 at 555; Simon Bronitt, 'The law in undercover policing: a comparative study of entrapment and covert interviewing in Australia, Canada and Europe' (2004) 33 *Comm L World Rev* 35 at 36; Andrew Ashworth, 'Should the police be allowed to use deceptive practices?' (1998) 144 *LQR* 108 at 108.

equal to modern experiences with miscarriages of justice. They do not chime with the insight that the principles observed in criminal justice are human rights and that their observance is necessary in any society that aspires to live under the rule of law.

Minimum standards of criminal procedure include the right to be 'presumed innocent until proved guilty according to law',[76] 'the right to a fair and public hearing by an independent and impartial court',[77] 'the right to examine the witnesses for the prosecution,'[78] and the right 'to the observance of the principles of natural justice', which is part of a wider 'right to justice'.[79] These rights are referred to in statements of rights, but indeed they were principles recognised as fundamental to the common law before they were put into such charters. They are part of the common law of jurisdictions which do not have enacted rights, such as most of the States of Australia.[80]

The right to fair trial underlies the integrity of the system of criminal justice. Lord Rodger and Sir Andrew Leggatt explained why that is so in a Privy Council appeal from New Zealand.[81] When trials are conducted according to

---

[76] New Zealand Bill of Rights Act 1990, s 25(c). [77] Section 25(a).
[78] Section 25(f). [79] Section 27.
[80] Only Victoria and the Australian Capital Territory have legislative statements of rights: the Charter of Human Rights and Responsibilities Act 2006 (Vic) and the Human Rights Act 2004 (ACT). The Constitution does not contain a statement of rights although the right to fair trial has been recognised to be implicit in it: see the discussion in *Ebner* v. *Official Trustee in Bankruptcy* [2000] HCA 63, (2000) 205 CLR 337 at [80].
[81] *R* v. *Howse* [2005] UKPC 30, [2006] 1 NZLR 433 at [44].

the common law and statutory rules for fair trial, 'people respect the verdicts because they have been reached in conditions which the law regards as fair'. In those circumstances 'observance of the rules . . . serves the wider public interests as well as the interests of the accused'.

The values and principles applied in criminal justice serve two general purposes. They minimise error in proof of guilt and they demonstrate observance of the rule of law. I make some observations about each of these two ends, because it is a mistake to take the view that the rules of procedure in criminal justice are rules about sufficiency of proof only. They are also minimum standards of fairness and decency required by the legal order.

(a) Fair Trial

The most developed rules of criminal justice have been rules of evidence designed to secure correct determinations of fact. For the most part, they are drawn from logic or common sense. The most important principle of proof is the inclusionary one that sufficiently relevant evidence is admissible. This, Wigmore's test,[82] is accepted in common law jurisdictions

---

[82] Wigmore described the object of proof as being to 'perform the logical (or psychological) process of a conscious juxtaposition of detailed ideas, for the purpose of producing a rationally single final idea': John H. Wigmore, 'The problem of proof' (1913) 8 *Ill L R* 77 at 80. He distinguished between what he considered were the two 'distinct parts' of evidence law (at 77): 'One is Proof in the general sense,–the part concerned with the ratiocinative process of contentious persuasion,– mind to mind, counsel to juror, each partisan seeking to move the mind

and in the enacted evidence codes or partial codes in which the rules of evidence are today often collected.[83]

Apart from the rules of evidence, the two principles which do most to shape the form of criminal justice are linked. They are the presumption of innocence and the bundle of interests usually referred to as the right to silence.

(i) The Presumption of Innocence

Perhaps the most famous sentence in English law is Viscount Sankey LC's declamation, in *Woolmington* v. *DPP*, that 'throughout the web of the English criminal law one golden thread is always to be seen – that it is the duty of the prosecution to prove the prisoner's guilt'.[84] The proof

---

of the tribunal. The other part is Admissibility,–the procedural rules devised by law, and based on litigious experience and tradition, to guard the tribunal (particularly the jury) against erroneous persuasion.'

[83] For New Zealand, see the Evidence Act 2006 (NZ), s 7. In Australia, uniform evidence legislation has been adopted in the Commonwealth, New South Wales, Victoria, Tasmania and Northern Territories jurisdictions: see Evidence Act 1995 (Cth and NSW), ss 55 and 56; Evidence Act 2001 (Tas), ss 55 and 56; Evidence Act 2008 (Vic), ss 55 and 56; Evidence (National Uniform Legislation) Act (NT), ss 55 and 56. The High Court of Australia has held that the uniform evidence code position on relevance 'reflects the common law' of Australia: *Washer* v. *Western Australia* [2007] HCA 48, (2007) 82 ALJR 33 at n. 4. The Canadian jurisdictions do not have comprehensive statutory evidence codes but the Supreme Court has explicitly adopted Thayer's similar formulation: *R* v. *Morris* [1983] 2 SCR 190 at [20]. The common law of England and Wales utilises a similar test: *DPP* v. *Kilbourne* [1973] AC 729 (HL) at 756.

[84] *Woolmington* v. *Director of Public Prosecutions* [1935] AC 462 (HL) at 481–2.

required, as everyone knows, is one that is 'beyond reasonable doubt'.

These principles were, however, insecure at the time of Maketu's trial in 1842.[85] (Indeed, they were not exactly secure in 1935 when *Woolmington* was decided.)[86] Mr Brewer may have reminded the jury that 'the humanity of the law of England always directs that the benefit of such doubt should be given in favour of the prisoner', but the principle he invoked was hardly expressed as the emphatic rule of today's presumption of innocence. Until the principles of proof and evidence were more developed in the course of the nineteenth century, it seems that Mr Brewer's claim for the benefit of any doubt was as far as the presumption of innocence may have gone.

The presumption of innocence, although part of the requirement of fair trial at common law,[87] is now recognised

[85] It took *Woolmington* itself to establish that the presumption required the Crown to exclude defences such as whether the gun had been discharged accidentally by Mr Woolmington, once some evidential basis for such a defence was raised. Lord Cooke pointed out that discharging such an evidential burden before an accused was able to give evidence (as did not occur in England until 1898) made this rule very harsh: Lord Cooke, *Turning Points of the Common Law* (The Hamlyn Lectures, Sweet & Maxwell, 1997) at 32.

[86] Lord Cooke in his Hamlyn Lectures thought that: 'A gaze at the web of the English Criminal Law would certainly not have revealed any such golden thread': *ibid*. Indeed, in *Woolmington* Viscount Sankey LC acknowledged that since *Foster's Crown Law* was published in 1762 'nearly every text-book or abridgment' had recited that, once it was proven that a person had caused the death of another, the onus was on that person to disprove malice: see at 474.

[87] See for example *Jago v. District Court of New South Wales* (1989) 168 CLR 23; *Dietrich v. The Queen* (1992) 177 CLR 292; *R v. A (No 2)* [2001] UKHL

as a human right.[88] And fair trial, itself a human right, is generally accepted to cover not only the proceedings at the trial in court itself, but the whole process of investigation, prosecution, and the public hearing to determine guilt, as Sir Anthony Mason and the European Court of Human Rights agree.[89]

Since *Woolmington*, it is clear that the prosecution must prove every element of an offence, including the necessary state of mind of the accused.[90] The presumption of innocence requires the Crown to dispel doubt as to any necessary intention or knowledge of the accused that is part of the offence.[91] When an accused may be convicted even if

25, [2002] 1 AC 45 at [51] per Lord Hope of Craighead; *R* v. *Griffin* [2001] 3 NZLR 577 (CA); *R* v. *Harrer* [1995] 3 SCR 562.

[88] Recognised by the International Covenant on Civil and Political Rights, Art. 14(1); European Convention for the Protection of Human Rights and Fundamental Freedoms, Art. 6; Canadian Charter of Rights and Freedoms, s 11(d); New Zealand Bill of Rights Act 1990, s 25; Human Rights Act 2004 (ACT), s 22; Charter of Human Rights and Responsibilities Act 2006 (Vic), s 24.

[89] *Jago* v. *District Court of New South Wales* (1989) 168 CLR 23 at 29; *Salduz* v. *Turkey* (2008) 49 EHRR 421 (ECHR).

[90] *Bratty* v. *Attorney-General (Northern Ireland)* [1963] AC 386 (HL) at 407 per Viscount Kilmuir LC.

[91] *Sweet* v. *Parsley* [1970] AC 132 (HL) at 150; see also *Brend* v. *Wood* (1946) 62 TLR 462 (Div Court) at 463 per Lord Goddard CJ; and *Beaver* v. *R* [1957] SCR 531 at 537–8. Subject to offences which are expressed as ones of strict liability, the requirement of *mens rea* (wrongful intent or with knowledge of wrongfulness of the act) is implied into statutory offences which in form describe only the acts or omissions constituting the offence. In *Sweet* v. *Parsley*, Lord Reid explained this requirement as the way that the law avoids 'the public scandal of convicting on a serious charge persons who are in no way blameworthy' (at 150).

35

the jury is left in doubt, there is a breach of the presumption of innocence.[92] While the defendant may be under an evidential burden to point to facts suggestive of mistake or other defence (a burden that is not inconsistent with the presumption of innocence), he does not assume the burden of satisfying the jury of guilt where there is doubt.[93] The presumption of innocence protects against error in criminal process. It is borne by the prosecution in proof of guilt in part because, as Brennan J of the Supreme Court of the United States put it, a defendant in such cases has at stake an interest of 'transcending value': 'liberty'.[94] But the public interest is damaged by error in criminal process too. The presumption of innocence maintains public confidence in the legal order.[95]

[92] As explained by Dickson CJ in the Supreme Court of Canada in *R v. Whyte* [1988] 2 SCR 3 at 18.

[93] *Woolmington v. Director of Public Prosecutions* [1935] AC 462 (HL); see *Proudman v. Dayman* (1941) 67 CLR 536 at 541 per Dixon J; as applied in *Sweet v. Parsley* [1970] AC 132 (HL) per Lord Diplock at 164; itself applied in *R v. Strawbridge* [1970] NZLR 909 (CA) at 914–16.

[94] *In re Winship* 297 US 358 (1970) at 364. The impact on liberty is not only in respect of the sentence imposed. Modern legislation imposes extensive restrictions on liberty for those convicted of a number of offences which may last for many years, or for life. For example, in New Zealand the Sentencing Act 2002 allows for the imposition of supervision and 'intensive supervision' orders on released offenders, and under the Child Protection (Child Sex Offender Government Agency Registration) Act 2016, a person convicted of a qualifying sexual offence must comply with onerous reporting requirements, in some cases for whole of life.

[95] *S.v. Coetzee* (1997) 3 SA 527 (CC) at [220], where Sachs J said: 'The starting point ... must be that the public interest in ensuring that innocent people are not convicted and subjected to ignominy and heavy sentences, massively outweighs the public interest in ensuring that

If a presumption imposed by statute compels a verdict of guilty even though a reasonable doubt exists, then the legal onus of proof is reversed.[96] That is so even if the factor in issue is expressed as 'an essential element, a collateral factor, an excuse, or a defence' (a matter often of drafting technique only).[97] It is 'the final effect of a provision on the verdict that is decisive'.[98] If an accused is required by law to prove some fact on the balance of probabilities to avoid conviction, the provision violates the presumption of innocence because it permits a conviction in spite of a reasonable doubt in the mind of the trier of fact as to the guilt of the accused. The presumption of innocence is subject to modification by statute only where the reversal is clearly enough expressed to overcome the presumption that Parliament does not remove such fundamental rights except by clear language.[99] Depending on whether the reversal of the onus is justified as a proportionate response to a pressing need, it may not infringe the human right to the presumption of innocence.[100]

a particular criminal is brought to book. Hence the presumption of innocence, which serves not only to protect a particular individual on trial, but to maintain public confidence in the enduring integrity and security of the legal system.'

[96] *R v. Whyte* [1988] 2 SCR 3.

[97] As Lord Steyn made clear when endorsing *Whyte* in *R v. Lambert* [2001] UKHL 37, [2002] 2 AC 545 at [35].

[98] *R v. Whyte* [1988] 2 SCR 3 at 18.

[99] As to which, compare the approaches of the House of Lords in *R v. Lambert* [2001] UKHL 37, [2002] 2 AC 545 and the Supreme Court of New Zealand in *R v. Hansen* [2007] NZSC 7, [2007] 3 NZLR 1.

[100] *Salabiaku v. France* (1991) 13 EHRR 379 (ECHR). And see the justifications suggested by Ronald Dworkin in *Taking Rights Seriously*

A reverse onus in regulatory cases or other offences not of serious criminal culpability (the touchstone suggested by Lord Steyn in *R* v. *Lambert*[101]) may be justified on public welfare grounds or on the basis of assumption of responsibilities which import obligations to provide information (as where a car owner must provide information about the driver, the required disclosure in *Brown* v. *Stott*[102]). But if reversals in the onus of proof could be justified simply by difficulties of proof or the seriousness and prevalence of particular offending, there would be little left of the presumption of innocence. The proof of absence of *mens rea* (the necessary intent or knowledge for a crime) might on these grounds be shifted to the defence in all cases, reversing the course the law has kept to since *Woolmington*. The presumption of innocence would then be relegated to 'relic status as a doughty defender of rights in the most trivial cases', as Sachs J memorably put it.[103]

The presumption of innocence compels a number of subsidiary rules of evidence. Its influence is seen in the exclusion of prejudicial information which is not sufficiently

(Harvard University Press, Cambridge (Mass.), 1978) at 200. He argued that there were only three grounds which could 'consistently be used to limit the definition of a particular right': if the values underpinning the right were 'not really at stake in the marginal case'; if another competing right would be abridged by applying the particular right in a certain way; or if defining the right to include the marginal case would lead to a societal cost 'of a degree far beyond the cost paid to grant the original right, a degree great enough to justify whatever assault on dignity or equality might be involved'.

[101] *R* v. *Lambert* [2001] UKHL 37, [2002] 2 AC 545 at [34]–[35].
[102] *Brown* v. *Stott* [2003] 1 AC 681 (PC).
[103] *S.v. Coetzee* (1997) 3 SA 527 (CC) at [220].

probative, a rule which addresses the risk that a defendant will be found guilty not on relevant and probative evidence tending to prove guilt of the crime charged, but on the basis of bad character. The extension of what used to be similar fact evidence and the frank acknowledgement adopted in modern statutory rules of evidence in a number of jurisdictions that evidence of propensity is probative and admissible are not always easy to reconcile with the presumption of innocence.[104]

The requirement that proof be 'beyond reasonable doubt' has been criticised as based on little authority and as being little more than a counsel of prudence.[105] It has, however, been hallowed by long use, particularly since the decisions of the House of Lords in *Woolmington* and *Mancini*.[106] And, although now sometimes buttressed by references to the need to 'be sure' or to 'be satisfied',[107] it remains the usual way in which the high quantum of proof required for proof of guilt of crime is explained. The view taken in common law

---

[104] C. K. Allen considered that propensity evidence had seriously eroded the presumption of innocence. He thought it was one thing to use it to rebut a defence accident or mistake, but 'a very different thing' to rely on it to disprove alibi or mistaken identity. He argued that the permissive attitude towards the admission of propensity evidence had made it 'idle to pretend that [a defendant] comes before the jury with a presumption of innocence in his favour'. See C. K. Allen, 'The presumption of innocence' in C. K. Allen, *Legal Duties and Other Essays in Jurisprudence* (Clarendon Press, Oxford, 1931) 253 at 291–2.

[105] *Ibid.* 253 at 288.

[106] *Woolmington* v. *DPP* [1935] AC 462 (HL); *Mancini* v. *DPP* [1942] AC 1 (HL).

[107] *R* v. *Summers* (1952) 36 Cr App R 14 (CA).

jurisdictions is that expressed by Brennan J in the US Supreme Court: 'a society that values the good name and freedom of every individual should not condemn a man for commission of a crime where there is a reasonable doubt about his guilt'.[108] The idea that the accused was entitled to the benefit of any reasonable doubt was clearly current at the time of Maketu's trial.

(ii) The Right to Silence

The presumption of innocence is closely associated with what Chief Justice Lamer of Canada described as 'perhaps the single most important organising principle in criminal law': 'the right of an accused not to be forced into assisting in his or her own prosecution'.[109] The privilege against self-incrimination was one acknowledged by the end of the eighteenth century.[110] Glanville Williams and, before him, Wigmore may have been wrong to ascribe it to the 'race

---

[108] *In re Winship* 297 US 358 (1970) at 363–4.

[109] *R v. P (MB)* [1994] 1 SCR 556 at 577.

[110] Wigmore puts it as beginning to be recognised by the end of the seventeenth century when the inquisitorial oath was abolished: John Henry Wigmore, *Evidence in Trials at Common Law* (McNaughton rev. edn, Aspen Law and Business, United States, 1961), vol. 8 at 289–90. Professor Langbein, in 'The historical origins of the privilege against self-incrimination at common law' (1994) 92 *Mich L Rev* 1047 at 1047 argues that its 'true origins are to be found not in the high politics of the English revolutions, but in the rise of adversary criminal procedure at the end of the eighteenth century'. He credits the rise of the privilege to 'the work of defence counsel'. In the United States, the privilege against self-incrimination was included in the Fifth Amendment to the US Constitution, which was ratified in 1791.

memory' of the Star Chamber,[111] but the right of the accused not to be questioned to obtain evidence of guilt was a strand of criminal justice which was invoked before even the presumption of innocence was secured. Its scope is, however, contested.

While a privilege against self-incrimination is not controversial, the consequence that adverse inferences may not be drawn from silence is not universally accepted.[112] It has been countered to some extent by legislation in a number of common law jurisdictions, although in some the scope for comment is much wider than in others. In England and Wales (but not in Scotland), the ability to comment or draw adverse inference from exercise of the privilege extends to pre-trial questioning by the police.[113]

---

[111] Glanville Williams, *The Proof of Guilt* (The Hamlyn Lectures, Stevens & Sons, London, 1955) at 39; John Henry Wigmore, *Evidence in Trials at Common Law* (McNaughton rev. edn, Aspen Law and Business, United States, 1961), vol. 8 at 291. In *Azzopardi* v. *The Queen* (1992) 177 CLR 292 at [118]–[124] McHugh J canvassed the modern research by Professor Langbein and others showing that the privilege against self-incrimination and the right to silence had been recognised much earlier than Wigmore had thought. For an explanation of how the different aspects of the right to silence developed at different times, see: Pat McInerey, 'The privilege against self-incrimination from early origins to Judges' Rules: challenging the "orthodox view"' (2014) 18(2) *E & P* 101.

[112] See Glanville Williams, *The Proof of Guilt* (The Hamlyn Lectures, Stevens & Sons, London, 1955) at 56–61, where Williams says that those who would prohibit the drawing of such inferences show 'extreme solicitude for the acquittal of the guilty'; and Glanville Williams, 'The tactic of silence' (1987) 137 *NLJ* 1107. See also E. W. Thomas, 'The so-called right to silence' (1991) 14 *NZULR* 299 at 320–1.

[113] See below at the text accompanying n. 120.

The objection taken in Maketu's trial to the fact that he had not been cautioned before being questioned at the inquest shows that the privilege against self-incrimination at judicial hearings was known and observed in New Zealand from the beginning. It is striking, however, that there appears to have been little exploration in Maketu's trial of the circumstances in which he came to make the out of court admission which was the principal evidence against him. It suggests that the implications of the privilege against self-incrimination had not been greatly developed at 1840. Certainly the right to silence had not assumed by that date a position as 'the single most important organising principle in criminal law'.

When defendants became competent to testify in New Zealand in 1889[114] (nearly ten years before similar reform was undertaken in England),[115] the legislation prohibited any 'comment adverse to the person charged', if he chose not to give evidence. That restriction survived in New Zealand until 1967[116] even though the English legislation from 1898 always allowed a right of comment to the judge. Since 1967 comment on failure to give evidence has been permitted in New Zealand, but from the judge or defence counsel only.[117]

---

[114] Pursuant to s 2 of the Criminal Evidence Act 1889. In Australia, the first state to enact similar legislation was South Australia in 1882. Victoria and New South Wales followed suit in 1891. Canada's legislation to the same effect was enacted in 1893.

[115] Criminal Evidence Act 1898 61 & 62 Vic c 36.

[116] When the Crimes Amendment Act 1966 came into force.

[117] Evidence Act 2006, s 33. Section 32 also provides that the fact-finder may not be invited to draw an inference that the defendant is guilty from a failure to answer a question or disclose a defence before trial, and the judge is required to direct the jury to that effect. Before enactment of s 32,

In Canada, neither the judge nor counsel may comment to the jury on the defendant's failure to give evidence.[118] In Australia, the uniform Evidence Act prohibits comment by the prosecutor, but not the judge or another party.[119]

a similar prohibition on such inferences except in 'exceptional circumstances' was enforced by the courts: *R* v. *Coombs* [1983] NZLR 748 (CA). Adverse inferences could, however, be drawn from the failure to disclose a defence pre-trial, even when the defendant had been told that he need not say anything: *R* v. *Foster* [1955] NZLR 1194 (CA). This could not be used to prove guilt, but merely as 'an answer to the defence' (*Foster* at 1200). In *Coombs* the Court of Appeal noted that this distinction caused some difficulty (at 751–2). It appears to have been similar to the current English system.

[118] Section 11(c) of the Charter provides that defendants have the right to not be compelled to testify at trial. Section 4(6) of the Canada Evidence Act RSC 1985 c C-5 prohibits the judge or trial counsel commenting to the jury on a defendant's failure to testify.

[119] The Evidence Act 1995 (Cth), s 20 provides that a judge or any party apart from the prosecutor may comment on a failure to testify, but (unless a co-defendant) must not 'suggest that the defendant failed to give evidence because the defendant had, or believed that he or she had, committed the offence'. The Commonwealth Act is the basis for the uniform evidence legislation that has been adopted in New South Wales, Tasmania, Victoria, the ACT and the Northern Territory. However, Victoria has moved the relevant provisions to s 41 of the Jury Directions Act 2015 (Vic), which requires the judge to give (on request from the defence or on the court's own motion) a more detailed direction prohibiting the drawing of an adverse inference. The Evidence Act 1906 (WA), s 8(d) and the Evidence Act 1929 (SA), s 18(1)(b) prohibit prosecutor comment on a failure to testify, but give no prohibition on adverse comments from other parties. A distinction sometimes drawn between inferring guilt from silence (an unacceptable infringement of the right to silence) and inferring the reliability of prosecution evidence which is not contradicted, at least in circumstances calling for an explanation from the defendant, has proved difficult in Australian case-

In England and Wales, s 35 of the Criminal Justice and Public Order Act 1994 explicitly permits the fact-finder to 'draw such inferences as appear proper' from a failure to give evidence and the power of the judge to comment on the absence of evidence from the defendant is preserved. In Scotland a judge can comment on the failure of the accused to give evidence in 'special circumstances' only. Otherwise the jury must be directed to draw no adverse inferences from a failure to give evidence.[120]

The ability to comment adversely on the defendant's silence and the recognition that the fact-finder may draw adverse inferences from silence at trial is supported by many because it is thought to reflect what any juror will actually be thinking.[121] The alternative view, put forward by Gaudron A-CJ, Gummow, Kirby, and Hayne JJ in the High Court of

law. For example, in *Weissensteiner* v. *The Queen* (1993) 178 CLR 217 the High Court of Australia held that (in jurisdictions like Queensland where there is no statutory prohibition on comment), it is appropriate in some cases for the judge to inform the jury to take into account a failure to testify when an explanation is called for, in that they can more readily draw inferences from the prosecution's uncontradicted evidence, but in *R* v. *Baden-Clay* [2016] HCA 35 at [51] the majority said that this applied only in cases where key facts 'were within the knowledge only of the accused and thus could not be the subject of evidence from any other person or source'.

[120] *Hogan* v. *HM Advocate* [2012] HCJAC 12, 2012 JC 307 has a useful summary of the law at [18]–[30]. In 2011 the Carloway Review recommended keeping the law as it is and not permitting the introduction of a general right to draw adverse inferences: Lord Carloway, *Carloway Review: Report and Recommendations* (17 November 2011) at [7.5].

[121] See above at n. 112.

Australia, is that it is not the function of the judge to instruct the jury on how to reason to a determination of guilt and that the jury should not be left to reason from silence to guilt because it is contrary to the presumption of innocence.[122]

Particular difficulty in drawing inferences arises when the defendant has invoked the right not to make statements when questioned by the police before trial. In England and Wales, adverse inferences from failure to answer police questions are now permitted under the Criminal Justice and Public Order Act 1994.[123] The position is the same (in trials for 'serious indictable offences') in New South Wales following legislation in 2013.[124] In other Australian jurisdictions, it is not permissible to offer evidence to support an adverse inference from exercise of the right to silence in police questioning.[125] In New Zealand, there is a prohibition on reference at trial to exercise of the right to silence when a defendant is being questioned by the police.[126] A proposal to remove the statutory prohibition was dropped at a late

---

[122] *RPS* v. *The Queen* [2000] HCA 3, (2000) 199 CLR 620 at [41]–[43].

[123] Sections 34–7. This legislation was enacted despite the contrary recommendation of the Runciman Commission: *Report of the Royal Commission on Criminal Justice* (Cm 2263, 1993) at [20]–[25]. See A. Ashworth and M. Redmayne, *The Criminal Process* (4th edn, Oxford University Press, 2010) at ch. 4.

[124] Evidence Act 1995 (NSW), s 89A.

[125] Under s 89 of the Evidence Act 1995 (Cth), Evidence Act 2008 (Vic), Evidence Act 2001 (Tas), Evidence (National Uniform Legislation) Act 2011 (NT), and Evidence Act 2011 (ACT). The uniform Evidence Acts reflect the common law as it still applies in the remaining jurisdictions: *Petty* v. *R* (1991) 173 CLR 95 and *Glennon* v. *R* (1994) 179 CLR 1.

[126] Evidence Act 2006, s 32.

stage of the Parliamentary processes, together with a defence statutory disclosure regime with which it was linked.[127] In Canada, exercise of the right not to answer police questions (whether under the protection of s 7 of the Charter[128] or under the wider common law privilege which does not depend on detention[129]) is not admissible because it is treated as irrelevant. Abella J said of adverse reasoning from silence[130] that 'since there was no duty on [the accused's] part to speak to the police, his failure to do so was irrelevant; because it was irrelevant, no rational conclusion about guilt or innocence can be drawn from it'.

This area of inferences from silence when a defendant is being questioned by the police is therefore one where common law jurisdictions are divided. The extremely difficult case-law in England and Wales has underscored the problems when the exercise of the right to silence is a result of legal advice.[131] It was described by the Carloway Review in Scotland

---

[127] See Criminal Procedure (Reform and Modernisation) Bill 2010 (241-1) (explanatory note) at 6–7. The modified Bill was enacted as the Criminal Procedure Act 2011.

[128] See *R* v. *Hebert* [1990] 2 SCR 151 at 194–6 per Sopinka J.

[129] *R* v. *Turcotte* 2005 SCC 50, [2005] 2 SCR 519 established that the right to silence at common law arose at any time when the accused interacts with a person in authority, regardless of whether or not he was detained or cautioned. The Charter right, by comparison, is triggered only on detention: *R* v. *Hebert* [1990] 2 SCR 151 at 184.

[130] *R* v. *Turcotte* 2005 SCC 50, [2005] 2 SCR 519 at [56].

[131] See *Condron* v. *United Kingdom* (2001) 31 EHRR 1; *R* v. *Hoare* [2004] EWCA Crim 789, [2005] 1 WLR 1804. In *R* v. *Beckles* [2004] EWCA Crim 2766, [2005] 1 WLR 2829 at [48], Lord Woolf CJ said that the issue of whether legal advice provides a good reason to not answer questions, and hence precludes the drawing of an adverse inference, is 'singularly

(which recommended against following the English reforms) as being of 'labyrinthine complexity'.[132] If there is to be an ability to comment adversely on silence when invited to offer

delicate' because: 'On the one hand, the courts have not unreasonably wanted to avoid defendants driving a coach and horses through section 34 and by so doing defeating the statutory objective. Such an explanation is very easy for a defendant to advance and difficult to investigate because of legal professional privilege. On the other hand, it is of the greatest importance that defendants should be able to be advised by their lawyer without their having to reveal the terms of that advice if they act in accordance with that advice.'

[132] In *Cadder* v. *HM Advocate* [2010] UKSC 43, [2010] 1 WLR 2601, the Supreme Court held that admissions obtained in an interview in detention where the suspect did not have access to legal advice could not be adduced at trial. The decision caused a furore, described by Lord Carloway in the foreword to his subsequent *Carloway Review: Report and Recommendations* (17 November 2011) at 1–2: 'The decision of the United Kingdom Supreme Court in *Cadder* v. *HM Advocate* had a substantial and immediate impact on the criminal justice system. The Scottish Government felt obliged to introduce emergency legislation to correct the flaws identified in the system's framework. The Crown Office abandoned hundreds of prosecutions, some of which were for very serious crimes. Significant uncertainty remained concerning the meaning of the decision. Several consequent subsidiary objections to evidence were taken in cases throughout the country, causing disruption and delay to court processes. . . . [T]he sudden over-ruling of previously well-established and accepted law is not the best way to bring about change in any criminal justice system. It leads to instant reactions rather than measured and thought-through plans for reform. It is highly disruptive to the system generally and has the potential to cause injustices in existing cases while attempting to redress perceived miscarriages in others. *Cadder* was a serious shock to the system. There is an acute need to ensure that, as far as possible, the system is not vulnerable to further upheaval as a result of a single court judgment. The underlying and long-lasting implication of *Cadder* is that the

an explanation, one thing that does seem clear is the need for adequate legal advice and time for it to be obtained and considered.[133]

The differences between common law jurisdictions suggest that Wigmore was right to point to a lack of agreement about the underlying policy for the right to silence and its justification. In part this may reflect an ambivalence towards the protections provided to a defendant in criminal justice. It may also reflect the lack of developed justifications in the case-law in a number of jurisdictions.[134]

(b) Rule of Law

A branch of law, like criminal justice, is not an island. It is, as Neil MacCormick said, part of 'an established legal order of rights and duties'.[135] Any such order itself 'has to be founded on some (however muddled and patchwork) conception of a just ordering of society'. This conception of a just ordering

---

system must fully embrace and apply a human rights based approach.' See at [7.5] for the rejection of the English system.

[133] That is illustrated by a recent case in the New Zealand Supreme Court: *R v. Perry* [2016] NZSC 102. A suspect's short telephone call with a duty solicitor from a roster maintained by the police (under the equivalent of the Judges' Rules) resulted in advice to say nothing until proper advice could be given. The suspect initially followed this advice but changed his mind after a police officer told him that it might not be the best thing for him to remain silent if he thought he was not implicated in the crime.

[134] Andrew L-T Choo, *The Privilege Against Self-Incrimination and Criminal Justice* (Hart, Oxford, 2013) at 10.

[135] Neil MacCormick, *Legal Right and Social Democracy: Essays in Legal and Political Philosophy* (Clarendon Press, Oxford, 1982) at 30.

of society is what we call the rule of law.[136] Although the rule of law is sometimes used as a 'self-congratulatory rhetorical device',[137] it is a necessary expression of the values that give legitimacy in a legal order that aspires to be a 'law-state'.[138] That is the sense in which it is referred to in the Universal Declaration of Human Rights and the European Convention on Human Rights. The rule of law has been said by the High Court of Australia to be a concept implicit in the Constitution of that country.[139] The preamble to the Canadian Charter of Rights and Freedoms recites that Canada is 'founded upon principles that recognize the supremacy of God and the rule of law'. And the rule of law is referred to as a constitutional principle in constitutional statutes in the United Kingdom and in New Zealand.[140]

The values in the legal order which are observed as part of the rule of law include those fundamental to criminal justice.

---

[136] Lord Bingham in *The Rule of Law* (Allen Lane, London, 2010) at ch. 2 traces the history of the concept of the rule of law and concludes that it 'came of age' with the Petition of Right 1628. That famous document remains part of New Zealand law (along with Magna Carta 1297, the Statute of Westminster the First (1275), the Bill of Rights 1688, and the Act of Settlement 1700) by virtue of the Imperial Laws Application Act 1988.

[137] Judith Shklar 'Political theory and the rule of law' in A. Hutchinson and P. Monahan (eds.), *The Rule of Law: Ideal or Ideology* (Carswell Legal Publications, Toronto, 1987) 1 at 1.

[138] Neil MacCormick, *Legal Right and Social Democracy: Essays in Legal and Political Philosophy* (Clarendon Press, Oxford, 1982) at 30.

[139] *Australian Communist Party* v. *Commonwealth* (1951) 83 CLR 1 at 193 per Dixon J.

[140] In New Zealand in the Supreme Court Act 2003, s 3; in the United Kingdom in the Constitutional Reform Act 2005, s 1.

Decisions of high authority in all jurisdictions have consciously invoked the rule of law as enforcing 'minimum standards of fairness, both substantive and procedural' in criminal justice.[141] Such values include in particular the presumption of innocence and the right to silence. Both are now recognised as human rights,[142] but they are equally fundamental principles of the rule of law. Statements of human rights contain provisions about the rights of those arrested or detained, and those charged, and specify minimum standards of criminal procedure.[143]

---

[141] For example, see *R* v. *Secretary of State for the Home Department, (ex parte) Pierson* [1998] AC 539 (HL) at 591; *Boddington* v. *British Transport Police* [1999] 2 AC 143 (HL) at 161 per Lord Irvine; referred to in *Siemer* v. *Solicitor-General* [2013] NZSC 68, [2013] 3 NZLR 441 at [206]; see also *R* v. *J (KR)* 2016 SCC 31 (which held that the protections in s 11 of the Charter were designed to protect the rule of law and fairness in criminal justice).

[142] International Covenant on Civil and Political Rights, Art. 14; European Convention on Human Rights, Art. 6; New Zealand Bill of Rights Act 1990, s 25; Canadian Charter of Rights and Freedoms, s 11; Charter of Human Rights and Responsibilities Act 2006 (Vic), s 25; Human Rights Act 2004 (ACT), s 22. As Sir Leslie Scarman pointed out in his Hamlyn Lectures, the development of statements of human rights in the post-World War II period (which included criminal process rights such as the presumption of innocence and the right to silence) were substantially the work of Anglo-American lawyers: Leslie Scarman, *English Law – The New Dimension* (The Hamlyn Lectures, Stevens & Sons, London, 1974) at 10–21.

[143] The International Covenant on Civil and Political Rights lays down minimum standards of criminal procedure for those in detention or charged with offences, including the rights: to be informed of the charges; to be brought before a court without delay; to challenge the lawfulness of detention; to be tried without undue delay; to be presumed innocent until proved guilty; to not be compelled to be a witness or confess guilt; to a fair and public hearing by an independent and

These fundamental values and human rights are not simply rules of evidence or proof. They are not only rules that have been adopted by the courts or by legislatures to promote correct decisions. They run deeper. In this way, Frankfurter J said of the development of the rules applied in federal criminal prosecutions in the United States that the courts in developing them had 'been guided by considerations of justice not limited to the strict canons of evidentiary relevance'.[144] It is therefore astray to see observance of such principles as part of the technical rules of a game which put 'blinders' on truth or aim to give criminals a 'sporting chance'. It is also wrong to suggest that the ends of criminal justice are to balance the rights of the individual not to be wrongly convicted of crime with the public interest in conviction of the guilty. The public

impartial court; to be present at trial and to present a defence either in person or with legal assistance; and also to appeal against conviction or sentence to a higher court. These rights are recognised in the New Zealand Bill of Rights Act 1990, the Canadian Charter of Rights and Freedoms, and in the European Convention on Human Rights, as incorporated into British law by the Human Rights Act 1998. Further rights are also recognised, such as the rights of those in custody to consult and instruct a lawyer without delay and to be informed of that right, and the right to refrain from making any statement and to be informed of that right. The New Zealand Bill of Rights Act 1990 (ss 24–7) also gives the right to the benefit of trial by jury if the penalty includes imprisonment for 2 years or more. Those charged have the right to legal assistance without cost if the interests of justice require it and if they do not have the means to provide for it. In addition, everyone has the right to the observance of natural justice and to bring judicial review proceedings or proceedings against the Crown.

[144] *McNabb* v. *United States* 318 US 332 (1943) at 341.

interest is in ensuring that the proof of guilt is safe and that the rule of law is observed.

Conclusion

James Fitzjames Stephen considered that criminal procedural reform occurred in England only when the state became less vulnerable following the upheavals of the seventeenth century.[145] Civilisation then flourished. Stephen is not the only lawyer to couple procedural protections for those accused of crime with 'civilisation'. In *McNabb* v. *US*, Frankfurter J, in overturning a conviction based on an improperly obtained confession, said that the 'minimal historic safeguards' of due process contained in the United States Bill of Rights did not fulfil the duty of the courts to supervise the administration of criminal justice through 'establishing and maintaining civilised standards of procedure and evidence'.[146] Such civilised standards, as the Supreme Court of the United States had emphasised before, were, he said, not 'confined within mechanical rules'. The end was not only to secure protection for the innocent, but also to secure convictions of the guilty 'by methods that commend themselves to a progressive and self-confident society'.

In our times, it is necessary to be careful that panic about crime does not erode the standards of 'a progressive

---

[145] See James Fitzjames Stephen, *A History of the Criminal Law of England* (MacMillan, London, 1883) at 416, where Stephen writes: 'The administration of criminal justice, after the Revolution, passed into quite a new phase.'

[146] *McNabb* v. *United States* 318 US 332 (1943) at 340–6.

and self-confident society'. Criminal justice comes to be considered today in a climate of anxiety, in which professionals, including judges and lawyers, are not trusted to have answers. The procedural law of criminal justice protects those who are not popular. It expresses values which are fundamental to fair trial and the rule of law and which are also human rights. They cannot be rationed in application to actual cases according to notions of utility or majoritarian preference without undermining the integrity of the legal order. These are conditions of some peril for the criminal justice system we have unless there is widespread commitment to the ends it serves and a willingness to allow it to evolve to meet changing circumstances, to the end that what is fair and just is done between prosecutors and accused.

Lecture 2

Righting Criminal Justice

In the Lectures in this series I discuss criminal justice, the law of procedure, and evidence applied in criminal cases in the common law tradition. In the first, I looked to the essential elements of the system we have in common. They include the distinct functions of judge, jury, prosecution and defence, and the principles developed, originally by judges, to achieve what is fair and just as between the prosecution and the defence.[147] In the final Lecture, I talk about the institutions through which criminal justice is delivered and the strains they face today. In this second Lecture, I concentrate on the linked principles of the presumption of innocence and the right to silence and their application in the investigation of crime and in particular police operations designed to obtain confessions.

The Presumption of Innocence and the Right to Silence

It has been said that 'if the average Englishman were asked what he considered to be the outstanding characteristic of English criminal law, or indeed of the whole legal system, he would probably answer without a moment's hesitation: "A man is presumed to be innocent until he is proved guilty"'.

---

[147] *Connelly v. Director of Public Prosecutions* [1964] AC 1254 (HL) at 1347–8.

And that he would 'almost certainly add, with no small satisfaction, that this was one of the numerous particulars in which the Briton had the advantage over the well-meaning but unenlightened foreigner.'[148] When Miss Hamlyn spoke of the 'privileges which in law and custom [the common people of the United Kingdom] enjoy in comparison with other European Peoples', it is likely that the presumption of innocence was at the forefront of the privileges she had in mind.

The rights commonly referred to as the 'right to silence' developed at different times and to meet different needs, but today they are seen as rights which give effect to the presumption of innocence.[149] The presumption of innocence was said by Laskin J of the Supreme Court of Canada to give the defendant both the 'ultimate benefit' of any reasonable doubt and 'the initial benefit of a right of silence'.[150] The initial benefit of a right to silence is necessary because if a defendant is obliged to assist the prosecution in making out the case against him, the presumption of innocence is undermined. The common law recognition of a right to silence was originally justified because until the end of the nineteenth century the defendant was disqualified from giving evidence and could not effectively challenge any statement attributed to

---

[148] C. K. Allen, 'The presumption of innocence' in C. K. Allen, *Legal Duties and Other Essays in Jurisprudence* (Clarendon Press, Oxford, 1931) 253 at 253.

[149] A matter that is discussed in the first Lecture; see above at the text accompanying n. 27.

[150] *R v. Appleby* [1972] SCR 303 at 317.

him.[151] When the prohibition was lifted by legislation, it was on the basis that the defendant was not obliged to give evidence.[152] The right to silence then came to be accepted as a stand-alone right justified not only by the original concern about reliability but by the more fundamental policy that it is not appropriate for a defendant to be conscripted against himself.

The presumption of innocence and the right to silence underlie the fairness of trial. Ensuring observance of the conditions necessary for fair trial cannot be confined to what happens in the courtroom. In common law jurisdictions today fair trial is understood to cover the whole process of criminal investigation and proof of guilt.[153] It includes fair treatment by police and prosecution. And it now includes access to legal assistance not only in the conduct of the trial but at all stages of the investigation.[154] Following adoption of

---

[151] See the explanation given by Lord Diplock in *R v. Sang* [1980] AC 402 (HL) at 436.

[152] The legislation making criminal defendants competent to testify (the Criminal Evidence Act 1889 in New Zealand; the Criminal Evidence Act 1898 61 & 62 Vic c 36 in Britain) provided that the defendant was not a compellable witness.

[153] See *Jago v. District Court (NSW)* (1989) 168 CLR 23 at 29 per Mason CJ; *Moevao v. Department of Labour* [1980] 1 NZLR 464 (CA) at 482 per Richardson J; *R v. Wichman* [2015] NZSC 198, [2016] 1 NZLR 753 at [193] per Elias CJ; *Cadder v. HM Advocate* [2010] UKSC 43, [2010] 1 WLR 2601 at [49] per Lord Hope; *R v. Collins* [1987] 1 SCR 265; *R v. Hebert* [1990] 2 SCR 151.

[154] In England, the right to consult a lawyer before questioning was recognised in the 1964 Judges' Rules: see *Practice Notice (Judges' Rules)* [1964] 1 WLR 152 at 153. In New Zealand, refusal of access to a lawyer was treated by the courts as a circumstance that could justify exclusion of

statements of human rights, the right to legal assistance is treated as closely linked to the human right of a suspect not to incriminate himself.[155]

Influences on Criminal Justice in the Common Law Jurisdictions

The common law of criminal justice has been heavily influenced in recent years by two forces. The first is the adoption of statements of human rights which restate minimum procedural protections for those in custody or being tried for criminal offences. The second is the capture in statute in a number of jurisdictions of the common law rules governing the admission of evidence and its exclusion for reasons of unreliability or impropriety in procurement.

Quite apart from those common law jurisdictions where statements of human rights are to be found in written constitutions,[156] statements of rights have been enacted in

---

any evidence obtained as unfair: *R* v. *Webster* [1989] 2 NZLR 129 (CA) at 135. The right to consult a lawyer is now expressed in human rights instruments (explicitly in the New Zealand Bill of Rights Act 1990 in s 23(1)(b), which also provides a right to be advised of the right to consult a lawyer)). It has been held to be implicit in the rights recognised by the Human Rights Act 1998: *Cadder* v. *HM Advocate* [2010] UKSC 43, [2010] 1 WLR 2601 at [41] per Lord Hope and at [93] per Lord Rodger.

[155] *Cadder* v. *HM Advocate* [2010] UKSC 43, [2010] 1 WLR 2601 at [43]–[44]; *Salduz* v. *Turkey* (2008) 49 EHRR 421 (ECHR) at [54]; *R* v. *Hebert* [1990] 2 SCR 151 at 173–5.

[156] Such as in the Constitution of South Africa or in the Canadian Charter of Rights and Freedoms.

New Zealand,[157] the United Kingdom,[158] and, more recently, two of the Australian jurisdictions.[159] The content of these statements of rights are generally comparable, although there are differences. They include, as minimum standards of procedural justice, the right to silence, the presumption of innocence, and the rights of those arrested or detained to have access to legal advice. All are components of the additionally recognised right to fair trial. Statements of rights differ, however, in the constitutional context in which they are placed. In Canada, the Charter of Rights and Freedoms is higher law as are the statements of rights contained in the constitutions of South Africa and Commonwealth jurisdictions which achieved independence following World War II. In other jurisdictions, rights are recognised by ordinary statutes and yield in the face of unmistakeable legislative limitation.[160] These differences impact to some extent on the methods of the courts and how the rights are realised in practice.

The recognition of the essential common law procedural rules of criminal justice as human rights gives them additional emphasis in the legal order. The implications of the 'righting' of criminal procedural safeguards are still being worked through. Although in the past the judge-made rules and practices of criminal justice have at times been viewed simply as a body of law concerned with rules of proof and fair

---

[157] New Zealand Bill of Rights Act 1990. [158] Human Rights Act 1998 (UK).

[159] Charter of Human Rights and Responsibilities Act 2006 (Vic); Human Rights Act 2004 (ACT).

[160] New Zealand Bill of Rights Act 1990, s 4; Human Rights Act 1998 (UK), s 4; Charter of Human Rights and Responsibilities Act 2006 (Vic), s 36; Human Rights Act 2004 (ACT), s 32.

trial, narrowly understood, their recognition as human rights confirms the earlier common law insight that they protect wider constitutional and rule of law values in the legal order. A possible consequence, not well developed to date in the case-law, is that the requirements of criminal procedure which are human rights tap into the deeper values that underlie statements of rights, in particular the dignity values which are behind modern statements of rights.

The second way in which the law of criminal justice has been transformed in recent years is through capture in statute of the important common law rules concerning the admissibility of evidence. Significant legislative reform and restatement of the common law of evidence has occurred in Australia and New Zealand and, on a less comprehensive basis, in England and Wales. In Canada, the law of evidence remains largely common law, perhaps making it more readily adaptable to meet changing conditions. The differences in legislative text and scheme across jurisdictions mean that some care has to be taken in the use of foreign case-law.

In Canada, breach of the provisions of the Charter compels a constitutional Charter-based response.[161] (In pre-

---

[161] Section 24(2) of the Canadian Charter of Rights and Freedoms provides that evidence obtained in breach of Charter rights must be excluded if 'the admission of it in the proceedings would bring the administration of justice into disrepute'. Public confidence in the system requires consideration of the seriousness of the breach (and the need not to condone state misconduct), the impact of the breach on the protected interests of the defendant, and society's interest in the adjudication of the case on its merits: *R* v. *Grant* 2009 SCC 32, [2009] 2 SCR 353 at [71].

Charter Canada judges had no discretion to admit reliable and probative evidence because of the manner in which it was obtained.[162]) In New Zealand, breach of the Bill of Rights Act fair trial standards was at first treated as setting up a presumption of exclusion but, following judicial retreat and legislative confirmation of it, that approach has given way to a general balancing of interests in each case to determine whether exclusion of evidence is proportionate to the impropriety.[163] The New Zealand legislation which now governs exclusion of evidence for impropriety, including breach of rights, modifies the pre-existing common

---

[162] *R v. Wray* [1971] SCR 272.

[163] The Court of Appeal reversal of the earlier presumption occurred in *R v. Shaheed* [2002] 2 NZLR 377 (CA). The former approach was adopted in *R v. Butcher* [1992] 2 NZLR 257 (CA); *Ministry of Transport* v. *Noort* [1992] 3 NZLR 260 (CA); *R v. Goodwin* [1993] 2 NZLR 153 (CA); and *R v. Te Kira* [1993] 3 NZLR 257 (CA). In *R v. Goodwin*, Cooke P indicated that 'good reason' to depart from the presumption of exclusion would arise in such circumstances as: 'waiver of rights by the person affected; inconsequentiality ... ; reasonably apprehended physical danger to the law enforcement officer or other persons; other reasons for urgency such as the risk of destruction of evidence; and the triviality of the breach if it is only a marginal departure from the individual's rights': at 171. For a comparative review, see Andrew Choo and Susan Nash 'Improperly obtained evidence in the Commonwealth: lessons for England and Wales?' (2007) 11 *E & P* 75. In the new 'balancing process', the court is directed to have regard to a number of matters. They include the seriousness of the offending, the nature of the impropriety, whether there was urgency in obtaining the evidence, whether there are alternative remedies, 'the nature and quality' of the improperly obtained evidence, and the seriousness of the breach of rights: see Evidence Act 2006, s 30(3).

law.[164] The approach taken under the uniform Evidence Acts in Australia similarly focuses on the impropriety. Exclusion of evidence is grounded on public policy, assessed in context in each case by balancing the interests engaged.[165] There is a further discretion to exclude confessional evidence if, 'having regard to the circumstances in which the admission was made, it would be unfair to a defendant to use the evidence'.[166] In England and Wales, s 78 of the Police and Criminal Evidence Act 1984 prompts a similar balancing of interests but against the standard of impact on trial fairness. The court must be of the opinion that the admission of the evidence 'would have such an adverse effect on the fairness of the proceedings that the court ought not to admit it'. The English legislation governing exclusion of evidence unfairly obtained is concerned with trial fairness, whereas the Australasian provisions place emphasis upon the proportionality of exclusion to the impropriety (although taking 'proper account of the need for an effective and credible

---

[164] So, for example, although New Zealand case-law before enactment of the Evidence Act had not weighed the seriousness of offending as a factor bearing on admissibility, it is now identified in the legislation as a consideration to which the judge should have regard. See *R v. Goodwin* [1993] 2 NZLR 153 (CA) at 171. Although not deciding the point, in that case Cooke P expressed caution about the Crown's argument that the seriousness of offending was a relevant factor. Similarly, earlier case-law that the good faith (or absence of bad faith) of the police was not relevant to admissibility is now overtaken by the statute which directs that the court may have regard to such considerations: see *R v. Narayan* [1992] 3 NZLR 145 (CA) at 149; and *R v. Goodwin* [1993] 2 NZLR 153 (CA) at 172 per Cooke P, at 202 per Hardie Boys J.

[165] Evidence Act 1995 (Cth), s 138.   [166] Evidence Act 1995 (Cth), s 90.

system of justice'),[167] and the Canadian Charter exclusion turns on whether the administration of justice would be brought into disrepute by admission of the evidence.[168] The extent to which these different approaches will lead to different outcomes in application is not easy to predict.

In addition to the discretionary jurisdiction to exclude evidence for unfairness, in all the jurisdictions I have mentioned the courts exercise inherent power to prevent abuse of their processes.[169] In England and Wales, the jurisdiction to stay cases to prevent abuse of process[170] is grounded in the public policy of protecting 'the integrity of the criminal justice system'.[171] It has been said to be a jurisdiction to prevent abuse of executive power.[172] The s 78 discretion to exclude evidence improperly obtained, on the other hand, is directed at the fairness of trial, which is treated as turning on questions of reliability.[173] Meanwhile, in

---

[167] Evidence Act 2006, s 30(2)(b).

[168] Canadian Charter of Rights and Freedoms, s 24(2).

[169] A recent example from New Zealand is *Wilson* v. *R* [2015] NZSC 189, [2016] 1 NZLR 705, a case concerning an undercover operation involving the use of fake court proceedings to give credibility to an undercover agent and an improper approach to a judicial officer.

[170] Following the decision in *R* v. *Horseferry Road Magistrates' Court, Ex parte Bennett* [1994] 1 AC 42 (HL).

[171] *R* v. *Looseley* [2001] UKHL 53, [2001] 1 WLR 2060 at [39] per Lord Hoffmann; citing with approval comments by Estey J in *Amato* v. *The Queen* [1982] 2 SCR 418 at 462–3.

[172] *R* v. *Horseferry Road Magistrates' Court, Ex p Bennett* [1994] 1 AC 42 (HL) at 61–2 per Lord Griffiths, in a statement approved by Lord Hoffmann in *R* v. *Looseley* [2001] UKHL 53, [2001] 1 WLR 2060 at [40].

[173] In *R* v. *Looseley* [2001] UKHL 53, [2001] 1 WLR 2060, the House of Lords held that where a stay has been considered because of abuse of process,

Australia and New Zealand, the power to prevent abuse of process has long been held to permit exclusion of evidence as well as stay of proceedings.[174] More recently in New Zealand, however, the Supreme Court has held that the assessment of whether admission of evidence would amount to abuse of process turns on a balancing by analogy with the statutory provision for discretionary exclusion of improperly obtained evidence.[175]

> 'if the court is not satisfied that a stay should be granted and the trial proceeds', state misconduct could be relevant to the exercise of the discretion to decline to admit unfairly obtained evidence under s 78 of the Police and Criminal Evidence Act 1984, but only if the evidence could not be fairly tested at trial: at [43].

[174] In addition to exclusion of confessional evidence not shown to be voluntary, the courts in Australia and New Zealand asserted a wider discretion to exclude improperly obtained evidence of any sort than was available in England and Wales or pre-Charter Canada: compare *Kuruma* v. *The Queen* [1955] AC 197 (PC); *R* v. *Sang* [1980] AC 402 (HL); and *R* v. *Wray* [1971] SCR 272 with *R* v. *Lee* (1950) 82 CLR 133 and *Naniseni* v. *The Queen* [1971] NZLR 269 (CA). In Australia, the approach taken in *Bunning* v. *Cross* (1978) 141 CLR 54 and *R* v. *Swaffield; Pavic* v. *R* (1998) 192 CLR 159 is now reflected in the Evidence Act 1995 (Cth), s 138. It provides that improperly or unlawfully obtained evidence is not to be admitted at trial 'unless the desirability of admitting the evidence outweighs the undesirability of admitting evidence that has been obtained in the way in which the evidence was obtained', taking into account a non-exhaustive list of identified factors. In England and Wales, a discretion to exclude evidence for reasons of fairness was not extended beyond confessional evidence until enactment of the Police and Criminal Evidence Act 1984: *Sang* provided that stays of proceedings (requiring a very high standard of impropriety) were the only way to deal with non-confessional evidence obtained via an abuse of process.

[175] *Wilson* v. *R* [2015] NZSC 189, [2016] 1 NZLR 705 at [60].

Exclusion of Confessions

Confessional evidence has always been treated cautiously by the common law. Before the arrival of human rights statements, common law courts protected observance of fairness in the obtaining of statements by exclusion of evidence and, in extreme cases, by staying cases where to proceed with trial would amount to an abuse of process.[176]

Confessions were excluded unless shown to be voluntary, that is to say not obtained through oppression or through an inducement or threat made by a person in authority. The general rule affirmed by the Privy Council in 1914 in *Ibrahim* v. *R* was that no statement by an accused was admissible in evidence against him 'unless it is shewn by the prosecution to have been a voluntary statement, in the sense that it has not been obtained from him either by fear of prejudice or hope of advantage exercised or held out by a person in authority'.[177] The principle was said to be 'as old as Lord Hale'. It was justified on the basis that 'a confession forced from the mind by the flattery of hope, or by the torture of fear, comes in so questionable a shape when it is to be considered as the evidence of guilt, that no credit ought to be given to it'.[178]

---

[176] See above at the text accompanying n. 169.

[177] *Ibrahim* v. *The King* [1914] AC 599 (PC) at 609–10; *Deokinanan* v. *The Queen* [1969] 1 AC 20 (PC).

[178] *The King* v. *Warickshall* (1783) 1 Leach 263 at 263–4, 168 ER 234 (KB) at 234–5.

That approach was followed in the other common law jurisdictions.[179] The limitation of the principle to inducements and threats given by a 'person in authority' was, however, more restricted than the statement of principle expressed by Lord Mansfield in the earlier case of *The King* v. *Rudd.*[180] He had treated confessions as involuntary both when coerced and when induced by 'threats or promises', without a requirement that the person obtaining the statement be someone 'in authority'.[181] Legislation in New Zealand now removes the common law requirement that conduct which could give rise to concern about the unreliability of a statement must be that of 'a person in authority',[182] but the 'person in authority' requirement remains in other jurisdictions and was decisive in the result in cases where confessions were obtained by undercover police officers, which I come on

---

[179] *Naniseni* v. *R* [1971] NZLR 269 (CA); *McDermott* v. *The King* (1948) 76 CLR 501; *Prosko* v. *The King* (1922) 63 SCR 226.

[180] *The King* v. *Rudd* (1775) 1 Leach 115; 168 ER 160 (KB).

[181] At 118, 161. See also *The King* v. *Warickshall* (1783) 1 Leach 263 at 263–4, 168 ER 234 (KB) at 234–5 per Nares J and Eyre B: 'A free and voluntary confession is deserving of the highest credit, because it is presumed to flow from the strongest sense of guilt, and therefore it is admitted as proof of the crime to which it refers; but a confession forced from the mind by the flattery of hope, or by the torture of fear, comes in so questionable a shape when it is to be considered as the evidence of guilt, that no credit ought to be given to it; and therefore it is rejected'. These cases were relied on by Kirby J in the High Court of Australia in his dissenting judgment in *Tofilau* v. *The Queen* [2007] HCA 39, (2007) 231 CLR 396 at [135]–[136] when explaining why he considered that the common law should not cling to the 'person in authority' requirement in the context of the undercover police interview there in issue.

[182] Evidence Act 2006, s 28.

to discuss. In a number of jurisdictions, including New Zealand, the rigour of the common law in excluding statements obtained by inducements was relaxed by statutory provisions that statements made following inducements were not to be rejected unless the judge was 'of the opinion that the inducement was in fact likely to cause an untrue admission of guilt to be made'.[183]

What Lies Behind the Caution in Relation to Confessions?

The caution of the common law in relation to confessions is in part because a confession is such powerful evidence of guilt and is sufficient in itself to justify a verdict of guilty. That is illustrated by the first trial held in New Zealand in 1842, which I discussed in my first Lecture. There a young Maori, Maketu Wharetotara, was convicted and executed wholly on the

---

[183] Evidence Act 1905, s 20. The original reform came in the Evidence Further Amendment Act 1895, s 17 (which had a slightly different test: whether the inducement was 'really calculated' to cause an untrue admission of guilt). The New Zealand reform was based on a Victorian statute: Law of Evidence Consolidation Act 1857 21 Vict 8, s 19. See *The King* v. *Phillips* [1949] NZLR 316 (SC and CA) at 339. In Canada, New Zealand, and the United Kingdom, the onus on the Crown to show that statements were voluntary was to the standard of proof beyond reasonable doubt, whereas in Australia it was on the balance of probabilities: see *R* v. *Ward* [1979] 2 SCR 30 at 40; *Rothman* v. *R* [1981] SCR 640 at 696; *R* v. *McCuin* [1982] 1 NZLR 13 (CA) at 15; *R* v. *Carr-Briant* [1943] KB 607 (CCA) at 610; *R* v. *Thompson* [1893] 2 QB 12 (CCR) at 16; *R* v. *Wendo* (1963) 109 CLR 559 at 562 per Dixon CJ, at 572–3 per Taylor and Owen JJ.

evidence of his confession. Wigmore thought that, if there was no doubt that a confession had been made, it was the very best evidence possible since 'no innocent man can be supposed ordinarily to risk life, liberty, or property by a false confession'.[184] Jeremy Bentham argued that 'the evidence drawn from the mouth of the culprit himself is always the most satisfactory, and the best fitted to produce in the public mind an uniform feeling of conviction'.[185] As a result of his belief that confessions were the most satisfactory proof, Bentham regarded the rule against questioning a defendant as illustrating an unfathomable reluctance to secure the conviction of the guilty.[186]

But Bentham's enthusiasm for the pursuit of truth through the defendant runs into the ugly fact of false confessions. It was the perception of the risk of false confessions[187] that initially led common-law judges to require the prosecution to prove that confessions were voluntary and not 'forced

---

[184] John Henry Wigmore, *Evidence in Trials at Common Law* (Chadbourn rev. edn, Aspen Law and Business, United States, 1970) vol. 3 at 303.

[185] Jeremy Bentham *A Treatise on Judicial Evidence* (Baldwin, Cradock, and Joy, London, 1825) at 245.

[186] 'If all the criminals of every class had assembled, and framed a system after their own wishes, is not this rule the very first which they would have established for their security? Innocence never takes advantage of it; innocence claims the right of speaking, as guilty invokes the privilege of silence': *ibid.* at 241.

[187] Illustrated by the eighteenth-century confession made under promise of pardon admitted at a trial of the person confessing and other parties to the same offence, recounted by Sir Alfred Denning in the first Hamlyn Lectures, where the 'murdered' man was later found to be alive: Alfred Denning, *Freedom Under The Law* (The Hamlyn Lectures, Stevens & Sons, London, 1949) at 29–30.

from the mind by the flattery of hope, or the torture of fear'.[188] The exclusion of evidence of such 'involuntary' confessions has continued to be part of the law, although today often channelled into statutory restatements which may not entirely preserve the breadth of the common law rule.[189]

Recent experience underscores the wisdom of the common law care about confessional evidence. The risk of unreliability in confessions is more serious than Wigmore thought. In a number of established cases of miscarriage of justice the evidence included confessions undoubtedly made that turned out to be demonstrably false.[190] A confession may have been made to put an end to police questioning. It may have been made to shield another. It may have been made because of the vulnerability and suggestibility of someone in police custody.

To former notorious but rare cases where supposed murder victims turned up unscathed years after a conviction[191] must now be added modern examples where convictions have had to be quashed because new methods of investigation have demonstrated that the confessions on which convictions were based were false. DNA analysis has led to exoneration of a number of those convicted after confessing to crimes they could not have committed, often after

---

[188] *The King* v. *Warickshall* (1783) 1 Leach 263 at 263–4, 168 ER 234 (KB) at 234–5.

[189] As discussed above at the text accompanying n. 161.

[190] The sort of experiences that led to the Runciman Royal Commission; see *Report of the Royal Commission on Criminal Justice* (Cm 2263, 1993) at [1]–[2].

[191] See above at n. 187.

years of incarceration.[192] The risks of false confessions are compounded by a tendency of police investigators to accept confessions at face value, limiting further inquiries or critical assessment of the admissions.[193] Admissions of guilt are treated as extremely powerful evidence. It is a commonly held view that no one is likely to admit to serious offending if not in fact guilty.[194] These are reasons why the known risk of false confessions is one that has to be taken seriously by any system of criminal justice. In some of these cases, the false admissions were apparently entirely convincing because they included incriminating detail thought to have been known only to the offender or because they were accompanied by apparently authentic expressions of remorse and demonstrations of emotion. A shocking example is the case of the five youths who

---

[192] See Gisli H. Gudjonsson, 'False confessions and correcting injustices' (2012) 46 *New Eng L Rev* 689 at 689; Brandon L. Garrett, *Convicting the Innocent: Where Criminal Prosecutions Go Wrong* (Harvard University Press, Cambridge (Mass.), 2012) at 18 and 295; S. Appleby, L. Hasel, and S. Kassin, 'Police-induced confessions: an empirical analysis of their content and impact' (2013) 19 *Psychology, Crime & Law* 111 at 113.

[193] S. Kassin, 'Why confessions trump innocence' (2012)67 *American Psychologist* 431; S. Kassin and others, 'Police-induced confessions: risk factors and recommendations' (2010) 34 *Law & Hum Behav* 3 at 23.

[194] Some studies involving simulated juries have indicated that confessions obtained in circumstances known to include violence are still treated as reliable: S. Kassin and H. Sukel, 'Coerced confessions and the jury: an experimental test of the "harmless error" rule' (1997) 21 *Law & Hum Behav* 27. See also D. Wallace and S. Kassin, 'Harmless error analysis: how do judges respond to confession errors?' (2012) 36 *Law & Hum Behav* 151.

confessed in 1989 to the rape and vicious beating of a woman in New York's Central Park.[195]

A number of risk factors for these false confessions have been identified.[196] They include promises or threats made by interviewing officers. Promises and threats were risk factors long recognised by the common law, which treated confessions made as a result of promises or threats as 'involuntary' until shown to have been otherwise. Lengthy interrogation and minimisation by the questioners of the offending are also known to raise the risk of false confessions. Those who are young and immature or have intellectual disabilities or who are socially isolated are particularly at risk of making false confessions in police interviews. Researchers also suggest that the structure of police questioning itself creates pressure to confess because it is confrontational and isolating of the defendant.[197] Some suspects have come to believe in their own guilt or, at least, to doubt their

---

[195] Described in S. Kassin, 'The social psychology of false confessions': (2015) 9 *Social Issues and Policy Review* 25 at 25–6.

[196] See S. Kassin and others, 'Police-induced confessions: risk factors and recommendations' (2010) 34 *Law & Hum Behav* 3; Gisli H. Gudjonsson, 'False confessions and correcting injustices' (2012) 46 *New Eng L Rev* 689; M. B. Russano and others, 'Investigating true and false confessions within a novel experimental paradigm' (2005) 16 *Psychological Science* 481. A useful summary of these studies can be found in *R v. Wichman* [2015] NZSC 198, [2016] 1 NZLR 753 at [393]–[399] per Glazebrook J.

[197] See for example: Christian A. Meissner and others, 'Accusatorial and information-gathering interrogation methods and their effects on true and false confessions: a meta-analytic review' (2014)10 *J Exp Criminol* 459; J. Pearse and Gisli H. Gudjonsson, 'Measuring influential police interviewing tactics: a factor analytic approach' (1999)4 *Legal and Criminological Psychology* 221.

innocence following extensive questioning.[198] Suggestions that 'speaking now' will be in the suspect's best interests and hopes of leniency have also been found to be significant in false confessions.[199] The increase in the risk of false confessions is a reason why it is necessary to be very careful of police investigative methods that cut corners or include inducements or do not scrupulously observe the procedural safeguards of criminal justice.

In addition to concerns about falsity, confessions obtained by the police are obtained in the exercise of public powers by those who are bound to give effect to human rights and who are obliged to exercise their public powers for proper purpose and fairly and reasonably. If what McLachlin J of Canada once referred to as the 'informed and sophisticated powers at the disposal of the state'[200] are not to be used as an engine of oppression, observance of the protections of the criminal justice system is essential to the legitimacy of the

[198] A. Memon, A. Vrij, and R. Bull, *Psychology and Law: Truthfulness, Accuracy and Credibility* (2nd edn, Wiley, Chichester (UK), 2003) at 79–81; see also Gisli H. Gudjonsson, and others 'The role of memory distrust in cases of internalised false confession' (2014) 28 *Appl Cognit Psychol* 336.

[199] A reason why the current pre-questioning caution required in England and Wales may be risky strategy. The caution is: 'You do not have to say anything. But it may harm your defence if you do not mention when questioned something which you later rely on in court. Anything you do say may be given in evidence.' See Home Office, *Revised Code of Practice for the Detention, Treatment and Questioning of Persons by Police Officers: Police and Criminal Evidence Act 1984 (PACE) – Code C* (The Stationery Office, London, 2014) at [16.2].

[200] *R v. Hebert* [1990] 2 SCR 151 at 176 per McLachlin J.

legal order. The procedural protections underpin the conception of a 'just ordering of society'[201] and express constitutional balances. The courts, too, are bound by human rights provisions. They need to ensure that in the exercise of powers to admit evidence improperly obtained the courts are not being used to perfect breaches of rights.

A further reason why particular care is required in admitting confessions obtained by deception is because of the direct impact on the human right to silence. That impact was the reason why in an early decision on the New Zealand Bill of Rights Act, the New Zealand Court of Appeal held that exclusion of evidence was the only appropriate response to a breach of a right such as the right to silence. Although exclusion of evidence was not necessarily appropriate in relation to other rights, such as the rights to be free of unreasonable search and seizure, exclusion was said by Richardson J in *Te Kira* to be 'particularly appropriate to confessions made without legal advice in a custodial situation'.[202] The 'inherently coercive effect of such a situation' made it likely in most cases that 'the confession resulted from the breach'.

Modern Policing

Perceptions of propriety in obtaining evidence have inevitably changed in response to changes in policing methods and

---

[201] Neil MacCormick, *Legal Right and Social Democracy: Essays in Legal and Political Philosophy* (Clarendon Press, Oxford, 1982) at 30; see the discussion in the first Lecture on p. 48.

[202] *R v. Te Kira* [1993] 3 NZLR 257 (CA) at 276.

evolving ideas of what is fair against the nudge of human rights. The requirements of fairness applied by the courts have also been affected by changes in technology. So, for example, the recording capacity which allows the filming of interviews with those suspected of crime and which has been required by rules of practice[203] has revolutionised criminal justice. Although the police were initially reluctant about judicial insistence that such recording should be standard, the great benefits of recording won them over. The taping put an end to dispute about the authenticity of what was said. It answered disputes about the observance of procedural safeguards such as the caution and the provision of information about entitlement to legal advice. The defendant's own words, as given, when admitted in evidence had much more impact than the laborious 'I said', 'he said' narratives recorded in notebooks and read out in court by police witnesses. And recording put paid to much argument about police inducements or threats, particularly when the right to legal representation was properly afforded.

It is difficult to know what is cause and effect, but there has also been a revolution in policing methods and attitudes. When I started out in legal practice in the early 1970s violence towards those in custody in the police cells was not uncommon. Nor was questionable police

---

[203] For example, Home Office, *Code E: Revised Code of Practice on Audio Recording Interviews with Suspects* (The Stationery Office, London, 2016); Home Office *Police and Criminal Evidence Act (PACE) Code F: Revised Code of Practice on Visual Recording with Sound of Interviews with Suspects* (The Stationery Office, London, 2013); *Practice Note – Police Questioning (s 30(6) of the Evidence Act 2006)* [2007] 3 NZLR 297, r 5.

behaviour confined to what happened in the police station. Sir Alfred Denning in the first Hamlyn Lectures illustrated the risk to deterioration in standards that is always present when people in authority believe that they are on the right side and that the end justifies the means. He told of a man charged with loitering on premises with intent to commit a felony.[204] The man's case was that he had got into a railway carriage on a siding not with felonious intent but simply to sleep. The policeman who found him acknowledged in answer to a question that the defendant did not have his boots on when found, substantiating his defence that he was intending to sleep in the carriage. The defendant was acquitted. A detective told the junior barrister who was prosecuting later, with what Denning says was a 'significant look', that if he had found the man 'he wouldn't have had his boots off'. In a similar way, as a young barrister I watched as a young constable, who had expressed some doubt when cross-examined about identification evidence, was after the case was dismissed immediately surrounded by older policemen and told off for not having been more confident in his evidence than was justified. Such attitudes and behaviour today are seldom encountered. That is I think because there has been a cultural shift in policing and much better discipline. Modern policing has become smarter and more effective. That is seen in the skilled harnessing of the huge advances in forensic science and investigative techniques.

---

[204] Alfred Denning, *Freedom Under the Law* (The Hamlyn Lectures, Stevens & Sons, London, 1949) at 25.

That is not to say that the modern advances do not bring temptations of their own and new collisions with values protected in criminal justice and under human rights statements. In the case of enhanced methods of investigation, for example, the capacity of modern surveillance caught the law unprepared. Until legislatures moved to provide authority for police surveillance[205] (in the UK following criticism in the European Court of Human Rights),[206] the courts in the UK and in New Zealand were at first prepared to accept that no lawful authority was required because the police possessed the freedom of action of all citizens if conduct was not prohibited by law.[207] When it became clear how much ground had been ceded and how extensive the potential erosions of liberty were, there was some retreat from the initial hands-off approach although closer supervision was not greatly developed before legislative intervention. In the case of phone-tapping and other forms of electronic surveillance, there is now legislative authority for police investigation which is

---

[205] In New Zealand, see the Search and Surveillance Act 2012; in England and Wales, see the Interception of Communications Act 1985, the Regulation of Investigatory Powers Act 2000, and the Investigatory Powers Act 2016; in Australia, see the Surveillance Devices Act 2004 (Cth) (this was preceded by several statutes regulating surveillance enacted by state legislatures). In Canada, see the Criminal Code RSC 1985 c C-46, s 487.01, enacted in 1993.

[206] In *Malone* v. *United Kingdom* (1984) 7 EHRR 14 (ECHR) at [79].

[207] *Malone* v. *Metropolitan Police Commissioner* [1979] Ch 344 (Ch). This was applied in New Zealand in *R* v. *Gardiner* (1997) 15 CRNZ 131 (CA) and the approach was reflected in the Court of Appeal's decision in the *Hamed* litigation: see *Hunt* v. *R* [2010] NZCA 528, [2011] 2 NZLR 499 at [43]–[49].

subject to inbuilt protections. The area of dispute today has shifted from lack of authority to whether its exercise was reasonable in the circumstances.[208]

---

[208] That still leaves unresolved, at least in New Zealand, whether public officials have the freedom of action of individual citizens, subject only to the limits imposed on them under human rights standards as to unreasonable search (which may be significant, depending on the scope of a space for what is private), or whether they are subject to rule of law or constitutional constraints: see *R* v. *Somerset City Council (ex parte) Fewings* [1995] 1 WLR 1037 (CA) at 1042 per Sir Thomas Bingham MR; and compare *R (New London College Ltd)* v. *Secretary of State for the Home Department* [2013] UKSC 51, [2013] 1 WLR 2358 at [28] per Lord Sumption JSC and at [34] per Lord Carnwath JSC. Also see *Hamed* v. *R* [2011] NZSC 101, [2012] 2 NZLR 305. In that case Blanchard, Tipping, McGrath, and Gault JJ considered the United States 'open fields' doctrine was inconsistent with the New Zealand Bill of Rights Act 1990, but Blanchard, McGrath, and Gault JJ found that the police surveillance of a place within public view did not amount to a search (see at [167]–[170] per Blanchard J; at [220]–[227] per Tipping J; at [263] per McGrath J; and at [281] per Gault J). In *Hamed* I considered that part of the rule of law requires that public authorities may do only what they are authorised to do by some rule of law or statute, and that police act unlawfully if they do not have specific statutory authority for intruding upon personal freedom (at [27]–[47]). In Canada, Bruce Harris records that the Federal Government 'is recognised as having all the powers of a natural person, in other words third-source powers': B. V. Harris, 'Government "third source" action and common law constitutionalism' (2010) 126 *LQR* 373 at 399, and see Peter W. Hogg, *Constitutional Law of Canada* (4th edn, Carswell, Toronto, 1997) at 15–16. In Australia, the executive authority of the Federal Government is derived from s 61 of the Constitution. 'In the light of the comprehensive authority provided by s. 61, recognition of the third-source authority for Government action is ambivalent': B. V. Harris. 'Government "third source" action and common law constitutionalism' (2010) 126 *LQR* 373 at 398. See also *Pape* v. *Commissioner of Taxation* [2009] HCA 23, (2009) 238 CLR 1 at

I do not here attempt to review the law on surveillance. Instead, I concentrate on the challenge for criminal justice values posed by modern policing directed at obtaining confessions of guilt. They bear directly on the rights to silence and to legal advice. With forensic science providing a spur for modern intelligence-led policing, it is perhaps not surprising that smarter policing methods have also prompted attention to the methods of obtaining admissions of guilt. And it is not surprising that much effort has been put into the sophisticated and extensive use of undercover policing operations (which has been a feature of modern policing since the 1970s) to obtain confessions. The opportunity for gain is most obvious when physical evidence of a crime is slight or non-existent but the facts are believed to be known to the person suspected of its commission or when the commission of a crime turns on the knowledge or intent of the defendant. Such opportunities provide temptations to push boundaries.

Police Questioning of Suspects

In the nineteenth century it was thought that a consequence of the right to silence was that it was improper for the police to question someone in custody following arrest. That restriction came to be relaxed over time, particularly after the rules of practice adopted as the Judges' Rules in 1912 attempted to impose some fairness in police questioning of those arrested

---

[126] per French CJ; and *Williams* v. *The Commonwealth of Australia (No 2)* [2014] HCA 23, (2014) 252 CLR 416 at [76]–[83] and n. 161 per French CJ, Hayne, Keifel, Bell, and Keane JJ.

or in respect of whom there was sufficient information to charge.[209] In the United Kingdom, New Zealand, and Australia, questions of fairness continue to be determined in part by reference to the Judges' Rules and their successor provisions in the different jurisdictions.[210] Whether the emphasis of human rights has sufficiently been taken on board in assessing questions of fairness is a matter on which views will differ.

Canada did not have equivalent rules of practice comparable to the Judges' Rules. Pre-Charter case-law took

---

[209] Compare *R* v. *Male and Cooper* (1893) 17 Cox CC 689 at 690 with *R* v. *Best* [1909] 1 KB 692 (CCA) at 693. In New Zealand, see *R* v. *Potter* (1887) 6 NZLR 92 (CA) at 96 where the Court held that it was the duty of the arresting constable not to ask questions. In *R* v. *Barker and Bailey* (1913) 32 NZLR 912 (CA) at 927, Edwards J said '[a]fter the police have resolved to arrest a person suspected of crime, or while he is under arrest, it is in the highest degree improper to question him as to any matter which directly or indirectly bears upon the crime in question'. See also the reasons of Williams J in that case, at 920. The shift towards a more permissive approach to police questioning following arrest, which is said to have occurred later in New Zealand than in England and Wales, is described by Richardson J in *R* v. *Te Kira* [1993] 3 NZLR 257 (CA) at 267–8.

[210] See in New Zealand the Evidence Act 2006, s 30(6), which provides that the Chief Justice's *Practice Note – Police Questioning (s 30(6) of the Evidence Act 2006)* [2007] 3 NZLR 297 is to be taken into account by a judge determining whether evidence was obtained unfairly. In England and Wales, see the Police and Criminal Evidence Act 1984, ss 66–7, which provides for the publication of Codes of Practice governing police questioning. In Australia, see Evidence Act 1995 (Cth), s 139, which provides for the cautioning of persons subject to police questioning. The Judge's Rules are used as guidelines in all Australian jurisdictions: see Andrew Ligertwood and Gary Edmond, *Australian Evidence* (5th edn, LexisNexis Butterworths, Chatswood (NSW), 2010) at [8.149].

the view that there was no discretion to exclude evidence that was probative because it had been unfairly obtained: a trial judge could not exclude a voluntary confession 'solely because he disapproved of the method by which it was obtained'.[211] Confessional evidence was not treated as an exception and was admissible even if unfairly obtained unless it was not shown to be voluntary. The adoption of the Canadian Charter of Rights and Freedoms, however, changed the common law and required evidence obtained in breach of rights to be excluded if its admission would bring the administration of justice into disrepute.[212] In the case of confessional evidence, the jurisdiction to exclude evidence for breach of rights remained additional to the exclusion of confessions not shown to have been voluntary.

As a result of the change brought about by the Charter, the Canadian Supreme Court in the 1990 case of *R* v. *Hebert* excluded evidence obtained by police officers acting undercover, who were planted in the defendant's cell, on the basis that the confession they obtained was obtained in breach of the defendant's rights to silence and to legal advice.[213] The ploy was found to have effectively denied the defendant his right to choose whether to speak, in breach of

---

[211] *Rothman* v. *The Queen* [1981] 1 SCR 640 at 666 per Martland J; see also *R* v. *Wray* [1971] SCR 272.

[212] Canadian Charter of Rights and Freedoms, s 24(2). Section 24(2) was intended to take a middle path between the Canadian common law rule in *R* v. *Wray* [1971] SCR 272, which required all sufficiently probative evidence to be admitted, and the 'American rule' of automatic exclusion: see *R* v. *Simmons* [1988] 2 SCR 495 at 532 per Dickson CJ.

[213] *R* v. *Hebert* [1990] 2 SCR 151.

his right to silence, and avoided the right to legal advice to help him in that choice. McLachlin J said of the right to legal advice that it existed 'to ensure that the accused understands his rights, chief of which is his right to silence'.[214] She took the view that to deny a discretion to exclude evidence for breach of rights 'runs counter to the fundamental philosophy of the *Charter*'.[215] Sopinka J in the same case said that the police could not prevent the application of the right to silence by 'disguising' themselves.[216]

When rights were breached it was irrelevant whether the statements were apparently reliable. Admitting improperly obtained confessions would be contrary to the courts' duty under s 24(2) of the Charter to exclude evidence obtained in breach of Charter rights, if its admission 'would bring the administration of justice into disrepute'.[217] The Charter 'had

---

[214] At 176. [215] At 178. [216] At 201.

[217] The principles on which the courts determine whether evidence must be excluded for breach of the Charter is discussed by the Supreme Court in *R* v. *Grant* 2009 SCC 32, [2009] 2 SCR 353 at [71]. McLachlin CJ and Charron J, writing for the majority, considered that, in considering exclusion under s. 24(2), 'a court must assess and balance the effect of admitting the evidence on society's confidence in the justice system having regard to: (1) the seriousness of the *Charter*-infringing state conduct (admission may send the message the justice system condones serious state misconduct), (2) the impact of the breach on the *Charter*-protected interests of the accused (admission may send the message that individual rights count for little), and (3) society's interest in the adjudication of the case on its merits. The court's role on a s. 24(2) application is to balance the assessments under each of these lines of inquiry to determine whether, considering all the circumstances, admission of the evidence would bring the administration of justice into disrepute.'

made the rights of the individual and the fairness and integrity of the judicial system paramount'.[218] In addition, the Court recognised that the state powers exercised by the police meant that the law of criminal justice was inevitably concerned with 'the superior power of the state vis-à-vis the individual who has been detained', thus drawing on deeper constitutional and dignity values.

In *Hebert*, McLachlin J took the view that the right to silence was linked to and was partly explained by the right to legal advice.[219] The right to silence was not only the negative right to be free of compulsion but a positive right to make a free choice as to whether to speak to the police. The way in which that choice was provided in the scheme of the Charter was through provision of the opportunity to take legal advice. The privilege against self-incrimination at trial, to be given full effect, required 'an effective right of choice as to whether to make a statement' at the pre-trial stage. A purposive approach was required to achieve the underlying value which the right was designed to protect. In a broad sense, there were 'two purposes': 'to preserve the rights of the detained individual, and to maintain the repute and integrity of our system of justice'.[220]

> The detained suspect, potentially at a disadvantage in relation to the informed and sophisticated powers at the disposal of the state, is entitled to rectify the disadvantage by speaking to legal counsel at the outset, so that he is aware of his right not to speak to the police and obtains appropriate advice with respect to the choice he faces. Read

[218] At 178. [219] At 176–80. [220] At 176 and 179–80.

together ss. 7 and 10(b) confirm the right to silence in s. 7 and shed light on its nature.

. . .the essence of the right is the accused's freedom to choose whether to make a statement or not.

Similar reasoning has been adopted by the Supreme Court in *Cadder* v. *HM Advocate*,[221] applying the decision of the Grand Chamber in *Salduz* v. *Turkey*.[222] In *Salduz*, the Court had recognised that the rights of a defendant 'will in principle be irretrievably prejudiced when incriminating statements made during police interrogations without access to a lawyer are used for a conviction'.[223] As Lord Hope and Lord Rodger both commented, the presence of the lawyer was seen by the European Court of Human Rights as necessary to ensure respect for the right of the defendant not to incriminate himself.[224] Further safeguards at trial could not remove the disadvantage of incriminating statements made without the benefit of legal advice as to whether to waive or invoke the right to silence.

It is not clear to what extent other jurisdictions will follow the repositioning occasioned by the recognition of procedural fairness rules as human rights, both in terms of direct breach of rights and in cases where the rights may not be directly breached but are effectively avoided. In a recent case involving undercover officers used to obtain a confession from a defendant in custody, the New Zealand Supreme

---

[221] *Cadder* v. *HM Advocate* [2010] UKSC 43, [2010] 1 WLR 2601.

[222] *Salduz* v. *Turkey* (2008) 49 EHRR 421 (ECHR). [223] At [55].

[224] *Cadder* v. *HM Advocate* [2010] UKSC 43, [2010] 1 WLR 2601 at [35] per Lord Hope; and at [67] per Lord Rodger.

Court followed *Hebert* in holding that the statements obtained by such 'active elicitation' were in breach of rights and had to be excluded.[225] In other cases not involving direct breach of rights but circumstances of unfairness which arguably undermined rights, the New Zealand Supreme Court has treated the reliability of the confession as of significance when considering the question of impropriety as required by s 30 of the Evidence Act 2006.[226] That is despite the fact that, before the Evidence Act, reliability of confessions was not determinative of exclusion for unfairness.[227] This emphasis on reliability has been explained in a recent New Zealand Supreme Court case as based on the scheme of the Evidence Act. It restates the common law rule as to inducements as one of reliability and was thought by the majority in the Supreme Court to relegate the discretion to reject evidence for unfairness to a residual category, available in exceptional circumstances.[228] It is debateable whether this approach will

---

[225] *R* v. *Kumar* [2015] NZSC 124, [2016] 1 NZLR 204.

[226] *R* v. *Wichman* [2015] NZSC 198, [2016] 1 NZLR 753 at [110].

[227] For example, see *R* v. *Wood* CA33/87, 20 March 1987, and T. J. McBride 'Evidence' [1989] *NZ Recent Law Review* 45 at 46.

[228] In *R* v. *Wichman* it was held that the scheme of the legislation (which contains a specific power of exclusion for unreliability and oppression) means that the discretionary power to exclude evidence for unfairness is a residual discretion to be used in exceptional circumstances only. The majority said '[s]ection 30 should not be treated as conferring a broad discretion to exclude defendants' statements for reasons addressed [in the sections dealing with reliability and oppression]'. It considered the availability but non-applicability of the provision dealing with oppression to be of 'significant contextual importance': 'the fairness analysis under s 30 will be in the limited compass of assessing police conduct short of oppression that has not led to exclusion of

prove equal to protection against evasion of rights or wider rule of law values. To date, too, there has been little attention in jurisdictions other than Canada to the policies that lie behind the right to silence. Kirby J, dissenting in the High Court of Australia, has, however, also expressed the view taken in Canada that the right to silence entails effective choice.[229] The present approach taken in New Zealand at least may leave a potential gap in protection of procedural rights in criminal justice in the case of undercover police operations where the suspect is not in custody (so that the human rights to silence and fair trial and the rules of practice concerning police questioning may not be directly engaged) and where the operation is designed to obtain a confession. These are circumstances which have been the subject of recent cases in Canada, Australia, and New Zealand.

'Mr Big' Operations

In the last few years the New Zealand Supreme Court has had before it three cases concerning elaborate police undercover operations, each carried out over many months. They seem to indicate a more systematic approach to what are called 'scenario' investigations.

One was a case of infiltration of a criminal organisation, a type of policing operation that is now familiar.[230]

---

evidence under [the reliability provision]': *R* v. *Wichman* [2015] NZSC 198, [2016] 1 NZLR 753 at [69].

[229] See below at the text accompanying nn. 254 and 270.

[230] *Wilson* v. *R* [2015] NZSC 189, [2016] 1 NZLR 705.

The courts have generally been prepared to accept this sort of policing as a necessary evil, despite the deception practised, because such operations are thought to be of public benefit as long as a line, hard to describe in advance, is not crossed. The same approach is taken to other deceptive police practices such as 'sting' operations targeting drug suppliers or fences of stolen property. The principal issue in the case that came to us was whether the use of bogus criminal proceedings – conducted by a court with the apparent approval of a judge, to give the undercover officer credibility with the gang – crossed the line, so that the prosecution of the gang members was an abuse of process. I do not describe that case further here because it was not concerned with obtaining confessions of past criminal offending but was, rather, the more usual undercover operation where the agent seemingly participates in the offending which itself becomes the subject of the criminal proceedings.

The second case concerned confessions obtained in a police cell by undercover police officers, acting as arrested drug dealers.[231] Significant preparation had been undertaken for the operation to enable the officers to establish a rapport with the defendant. One officer was brought in because he was of the same ethnicity as the defendant. Planning for the operation had taken more than a day but seems to have been kept from the officer who was dealing with the defendant and in communication with his lawyer, after the defendant had asked to consult a lawyer before continuing with a police interview. The lawyer had arranged with the officer to see the defendant the next day and

---

[231] *R v. Kumar* [2015] NZSC 124, [2016] 1 NZLR 204.

had been given the impression that no attempt would be made by the police to question the client further in the meantime. It was a matter of some moment to the senior officer who deployed the undercover operation that no explicit undertaking not to ask further questions had been given. The undercover officers were placed in the cell with the defendant and through skilful and persistent questioning elicited incriminating statements from him. The Supreme Court excluded the statements as having been obtained in breach of rights.

The third operation was conducted by what the New Zealand Police call the 'Crime Scenario Undercover Technique'.[232] The operation was designed to obtain a confession of past offending. The defendant was not in custody or under arrest. The crime being investigated had occurred three years earlier. The technique drew the defendant into an apparent criminal organisation over a period of some months. It was designed to culminate in an interview with the 'boss' of the organisation. The interview was represented to be the last hurdle to be cleared by the defendant to enable him to be accepted as a full member of the organisation. In fact, the whole purpose of the operation was to obtain a confession of guilt at the interview.

The method does not entail direct breach of provisions of the Bill of Rights, because the suspect is not in custody.[233] Such investigations have been called 'Mr Big'

[232] *R v. Wichman* [2015] NZSC 198, [2016] 1 NZLR 753.
[233] The rights in s 23 of the New Zealand Bill of Rights Act 1990 only apply to persons 'arrested or . . . detained under any enactment'. The Chief Justice's *Practice Note – Police Questioning (s 30(6) of the Evidence Act 2006)* [2007] 3 NZLR 297, r 2, requires a caution to be given once sufficient evidence exists to charge the person being questioned.

operations, because of the importance of the role played by the head of the organisation. The investigation is patterned on a Canadian model. Its formula was summarised in a 2014 decision of the Canadian Supreme Court:[234]

> Over a period of weeks or months, suspects are made to believe that the fictitious criminal organization for which they work can provide them with financial security, social acceptance, and friendship. Suspects also come to learn that violence is a necessary part of the organization's business model, and that a past history of violence is a boast-worthy accomplishment. And during the final meeting with Mr. Big – which involves a skilful interrogation conducted by an experienced police officer – suspects learn that confessing to the crime under investigation provides a consequence-free ticket into the organization and all of the rewards it provides.

The technique as applied in New Zealand follows this model with the important modification that violence is not part of the enacted scenarios, although there may be an element of

In *R v. Wichman* [2015] NZSC 198, [2016] 1 NZLR 753, the Court divided on the question of whether the *Practice Note* applies to Mr Big-style operations, with the majority holding that it did not: see at [106] per William Young, Arnold, and O'Regan JJ, at [318] per Elias CJ, and at [474]–[476] per Glazebrook J. In England and Wales, a caution must be given prior to questioning of a 'person whom there are grounds to suspect of an offence' if their answers or silence can be used as evidence in court: Home Office, *Revised Code of Practice for the Detention, Treatment and Questioning of Persons by Police Officers: Police and Criminal Evidence Act 1984 (PACE) – Code C* (The Stationery Office, London, 2014) at [10.1].

[234] *R v. Hart* 2014 SCC 52, [2014] 2 SCR 544 at [68].

menace from the circumstances of the criminal activity of the organisation.

The operation is an elaborate undercover deception designed to obtain confessions of past offending. Scenario undercover operations are expensive and may involve dozens of undercover agents sometimes over a period of many months.[235] Such operations are used for serious crime, often involving 'cold' cases. The suspect is drawn into what seems to be a criminal organisation through an apparently chance encounter with one of the undercover police officers. Over a period of months the person is involved in a number of staged 'scenarios' in which he is given jobs to undertake for the organisation of a shady or criminal nature, such as repossessions or stand-over debt collection. Over time the seriousness of the apparent offending may escalate. The operations vary because they are targeted at the particular suspect. They may be designed with input from a psychologist, as the New Zealand operation was.

In the case dealt with by the New Zealand Supreme Court, *R* v. *Wichman*, the police suspected that the defendant, when 17 years old, had caused fatal injuries to his baby, a twin, by shaking her when she would not stop crying.[236] He had at the time acknowledged shaking the child, but said it had been in an attempt to resuscitate her after she had stopped breathing. The operation was launched three years later.

---

[235] See Kouri T. Keenan and Joan Brockman, *Mr. Big: Exposing Undercover Investigations in Canada* (Fernwood, Halifax (Nova Scotia), 2010) at 23; and *R* v. *Wichman* [2015] NZSC 198, [2016] 1 NZLR 753 at [17].

[236] *R* v. *Wichman* [2015] NZSC 198, [2016] 1 NZLR 753.

The design of the operation is to make the suspect believe himself to be befriended by members of the organisation. Through the enacted scenarios he is made to become dependent on the organisation and anxious to become a full member of it. In the actual case, the suspect received some payment for the work he was given to perform (of apparently escalating criminal seriousness) but the prospect of more lucrative opportunities, a glamorous lifestyle, and friendships with the other members was dangled before him as something he could expect if admitted as a full member of the organisation. The suspect in the case was encouraged to lose weight and dress smartly and his self-esteem was consciously boosted. As was part of the design, he was told that the key to becoming a member was the impression he made on its boss, someone he would meet towards the end of the operation. He was told repeatedly that the organisation insisted on total trust, loyalty, and truthfulness and that his acceptance would depend on whether the boss was convinced he had those qualities.

In a typical Mr Big operation the suspect will have been led to understand that the boss has corrupt police on his payroll and is able to get rid of any difficulties with the law that a member of the organisation may have, just as long as the person is honest about the problems he has. There may be a scenario designed to demonstrate how problems with the police have been cleared away for other members of the organisation, if the boss intervenes. In the particular case before the Supreme Court the suspect was involved in the delivery of a stolen passport to be used in the flight of a member of the organisation who was being investigated by the police for sexual offending against young girls. He was told that, had the member sought help earlier, the boss would have been able to see that the charges were taken care of. Typically, shortly before the interview with the boss is to take place, some step will be taken by the police in relation to the crime which is the real undisclosed subject of the operation, to create anxiety in the mind of the suspect about it. In the *Wichman* case, a member of the police contacted the suspect's family to advise them that the inquest into the death of the baby was about to reconvene. Intercepted phone calls between the suspect and his girlfriend, the mother of the twins, indicated that they expected he would be charged in connection with the death.

At the interview with the boss, the suspect will be led to believe that he will be admitted to the organisation if he passes the test of demonstrating truthfulness and loyalty. It will also be suggested to him that the criminal investigation may be able to be halted by the boss's intervention. The interview is turned by the boss to the offending, perhaps on the basis that the boss has learned through his contacts in the police that the suspect has some unresolved trouble and he needs to know about it so that it can be fixed because the organisation cannot afford to have unresolved police investigations into one of its members. The interviewing on the point is persistent. The boss does not accept exculpatory statements and is insistent that he must be told the truth. During the course of such interviews denials on the critical questions are met with expressions of disbelief. There are therefore incentives on the suspect to tell the interviewer what he wants to hear, particularly as it seems that confessions in such a setting are costless, because of the loyalty practised by the organisation. There is also the hoped-for advantage that the organisation will make the risk of criminal prosecution disappear.

The course of the interview may, as in the *Wichman* case, mimic aspects of a police interview. Wichman was told at an early stage of the interview that the door was open and that if he did not want to continue with the interview he just had to leave and there would be no hard feelings. He was asked whether he was happy to be speaking to the boss about the matters raised. On the other hand, the interview was persistent and entailed cross-examination and minimisation of moral blameworthiness in a way which would not be countenanced in a frank police interview. In the *Wichman* case, judges remarked upon the emphasis placed in the interview upon the need for truth as a value of the organisation and the indications that the defendant does not need to go through with the interview if he does not want to, giving some comfort in terms of the reliability of the statements.[237] This may be dangerous reasoning in the artificial world created by the operation.

The features of the interrogation (the apparent lack of cost to the defendant of any admissions made, the incentives of gaining admission to the organisation and relief from the risk of prosecution, and the minimisation of culpability) are all features which are known to raise the

---

[237] See *R* v. *Wichman* [2013] NZHC 3260 at [34] and [70]; and *R* v. *Wichman* [2015] NZSC 198, [2016] 1 NZLR 753 at [87].

risk of false confessions. Some false confessions have been reported arising out of the Canadian Mr Big operations.[238] Since the whole purpose of the Mr Big operations is to obtain confessions, the methods are 'carefully calibrated to achieve that end', as the Supreme Court of Canada has recognised in *Hart*.[239] In the distorted reality which the scenarios set up, the defendant's true freedom of choice to make a statement is whittled away.

The scenario technique has been extremely successful. In Canada, it has been reported that 75 per cent of operations are successful in either leading to charges or having suspects cleared. Of cases that result in prosecution, 95 per cent have resulted in convictions.[240] In New Zealand, the scale of operations has not been as extensive as in Canada but the results seem to be equally effective, particularly in cold cases. In two cases, Mr Big operations resulted in successful prosecutions for murder and the recovery of the bodies of the victims after many years.[241]

---

[238] They are mentioned in *R* v. *Hart* 2014 SCC 52, [2014] 2 SCR 544 at [62]; and see Bruce A. MacFarlane, 'Wrongful convictions: determining culpability when the sand keeps shifting' (2014) 47 *UBC L Rev* 597 at 615–16.

[239] *R* v. *Hart* 2014 SCC 52, [2014] 2 SCR 544 at [68].

[240] See Royal Canadian Mounted Police, 'Undercover operations: questions and answers', available at: www.rcmp-grc.gc.ca (last accessed 9 November 2016).

[241] See *R* v. *Reddy* [2016] NZHC 1294, [2016] 3 NZLR 666. That decision concerned an unsuccessful post-trial application for suppression of details of the technique.

'Mr Big' in Court

Mr Big operations have been before the final courts in Canada, Australia, and New Zealand. The cases and the courts have been divided. And in Canada at least there has been a change of heart by the courts. In a 2005 case, *R v. Grandinetti*, the Supreme Court of Canada took the view that the undercover agent, who, as Mr Big, offered the usual inducements in such operations of being able to make a police investigation go away and membership of the organisation, was not a 'person in authority' for the purposes of the common law rule relating to inducements.[242] In 2014, however, the Supreme Court revisited *Grandinetti* and took the view that its earlier approach provided insufficient protection for those targeted in a Mr Big operation. The Supreme Court in *R v. Hart* recognised that there is collateral prejudice in the use of statements obtained in the circumstances of a Mr Big operation.[243] The combination of questions about reliability and prejudice from the inevitable inference of bad character based on willingness to participate in a criminal organisation is a 'potent mix' and increases the risk of wrongful conviction.[244] More importantly, the Mr Big technique had highlighted a loophole in the protection provided by the Charter.[245] It applied only to those in custody. In a scenario operation the defendant is not in police custody but is, instead, drawn into a 'virtual world' for the purposes of obtaining a confession.

---

[242] *R v. Grandinetti* 2005 SCC 5, [2005] 1 SCR 27.
[243] *R v. Hart* 2014 SCC 52, [2014] 2 SCR 544.   [244] *Ibid.* at [8].
[245] *Ibid.* at [79].

The Court moved to fill this gap by the creation of a new common law rule of exclusion and by a 'reinvigorated' doctrine of abuse of process.[246]

Under the new common law rule developed by the Canadian Supreme Court in *Hart*, a confession obtained by such police deception is presumptively inadmissible unless the Crown establishes on a balance of probabilities that the probative value of the confession outweighs its prejudicial effect. The additional, 'more robust', approach to abuse of process means that the evidence obtained will be excluded when the police tactics approach coercion by overcoming the will of the accused.[247] In considering coercion, the Court made it clear that operations may become coercive in ways other than violence or threats of violence: 'Operations that prey on an accused's vulnerabilities – like mental health problems, substance addictions, or youthfulness – are also highly problematic':[248]

> Taking advantage of these vulnerabilities threatens trial fairness and the integrity of the justice system. As this Court has said on many occasions, misconduct that offends the community's sense of fair play and decency will amount to an abuse of process and warrant the exclusion of the statement.

In *Hart* itself, the confession was excluded because the social isolation of the defendant and the transformation of his life as a result of the operation meant that the inducement to confess was powerful. Nor was there any confirmatory evidence as to

---

[246] At [114].   [247] At [84].   [248] At [117].

the reliability of the statement. By contrast, in another case decided at the same time, the lower level of inducements and the presence of cogent confirmatory evidence in the discovery of the remains of the victim led to a conclusion that the confession should be admitted.[249]

The High Court of Australia applied *Grandinetti* in a 2007 case, *Tofilau*, which held that the technique did not engage the common law prohibitions on admission of confessions not shown to be voluntary or for unfairness.[250] The majority considered that the inducement or threat in the Mr Big operation was not made by a person in authority because the undercover officer was not known to the suspect to be a police officer.[251] Nor was there any coercion or overbearing of the suspect's will because of the advantage hoped for or the deception of the police.[252] *Tofilau* was decided before the reconsideration of *Grandinetti* by the Supreme Court of Canada in *Hart*. It is also not easy to reconcile with an earlier decision of the High Court.[253] And it was a case which produced a strong dissenting judgment from Kirby J. He emphasised the dangers of applying language from earlier cases to a policing technique that could not have been imagined at the time. He thought that in addressing the challenges of

---

[249] *R v. Mack* 2014 SCC 58, [2014] 3 SCR 3.
[250] *Tofilau v. The Queen* [2007] HCA 39, (2007) 231 CLR 396.
[251] At [13] per Gleeson CJ, [29] per Gummow and Hayne JJ, and [323] per Callinan, Heydon, and Crennan JJ.
[252] At [22] per Gleeson CJ, [81] per Gummow and Hayne JJ, and [369] per Callinan, Heydon, and Crennan JJ.
[253] *R v. Swaffield; Pavic v. R* (1998) 192 CLR 159.

the scenario policing technique it was necessary to start with the long-standing caution of the common law about confessional evidence:[254]

> To the extent that the law demands that the recipient of a confession must not only *in fact* be a 'person in authority' (such as a police officer or prosecutor), but must be *known* to be such by the suspect and must have, and be known to have, *lawful* power to influence the course of criminal proceedings, the ambit of the protection of the inducement rule is obviously diminished. Its capacity to restrain the use of confessional evidence that is 'involuntary', in the sense of being affected by a relevant hope or fear, is reduced. Very good reasons would be needed to confine the inducement rule in such a way.

In the New Zealand Mr Big case which reached the Supreme Court, *Wichman*, the appeal was argued on the basis that the confession should be excluded as having been unfairly obtained.[255] It was not argued that it was unreliable and should be excluded under the provision of the Evidence Act which replaces the inducement arm of the common law exclusion for involuntariness (for cases not amounting to oppression).[256] By majority, the Supreme Court held that the

---

[254] *Tofilau v. The Queen* [2007] HCA 39, (2007) 231 CLR 396 at [140].

[255] *R v. Wichman* [2015] NZSC 198, [2016] 1 NZLR 753.

[256] In dissent, I would have treated the statement as inadmissible because unreliable within the meaning of s 28 of the Evidence Act 2006 because the circumstances in which the statement was made raised concerns about reliability which I considered had not been excluded. The majority position that the statement was reliable (a conclusion of the High Court, in which s 28 was in issue, from which the majority did not depart) would

evidence was admissible, finding it was not unfairly obtained. Critical to this determination was the view reached by the majority that the evidence was reliable evidence of guilt. The question of reliability was assessed by considering the internal consistency of the statement, its consistency with the known facts, and the apparently 'cathartic' effect the decision to speak had on the defendant.[257] I dissented from the result and would have upheld the Court of Appeal, which had unanimously rejected the confession as unfairly obtained.[258] Following the delivery of the judgment of the Supreme Court, the defendant pleaded guilty to manslaughter.

The courts in England and Wales have not had to grapple directly with confessions obtained in a Mr Big operation. Although incriminating statements were made in the course of an undercover fencing operation in *R* v. *Christou*,[259] the operation was not set up to obtain confessions and the information provided was in the course of the sort of 'banter' that was part of the cover for the operation. No inducements or incentives to confess were offered. Even so, the Court of Appeal expressed the view that it would be wrong for an undercover disguise to be used to enable police officers to ask questions

---

also have made exclusion under s 28 much less likely given the majority's conclusion that an assessment of the confession's truth is relevant to that rule.

[257] See *R* v. *Wichman* [2013] NZHC 3260 at [80]–[86]. The Supreme Court majority did not depart from the High Court Judge's conclusion on the statement's reliability: see *R* v. *Wichman* [2015] NZSC 198, [2016] 1 NZLR 753 at [93].

[258] *Wichman* v. *R* [2014] NZCA 339, [2015] 2 NZLR 137.

[259] *R* v. *Christou* [1992] QB 979 (CA).

about an offence 'uninhibited by the requirements of the Code [under PACE] and with the effect of circumventing it'.[260] In the same vein, the Court of Appeal in *R* v. *Whiteley* drew a distinction between the case where an undercover agent seeks to obtain evidence about a past offence, where the Code as to interviews must be complied with, and the case where an undercover officer seeks to find out whether the person approached is prepared to commit a crime (in that case, by supplying heroin).[261]

Although the English courts have not had to consider a Mr Big operation in a domestic context, a Mr Big Canadian confession was in issue in an extradition matter in *R* v. *Bow Street Magistrates' Court, ex parte Proulx*.[262] In that case the Divisional Court indicated that, if the evidence had been put forward 'in a purely domestic context', it might have faced 'considerable difficulty'.[263] Since the context was extradition, Mance LJ considered that the matter was different. The first instance Court's reliance on the evidence could not be said to have 'outrag[ed] civilised values', justifying the Court interfering with the decision on appeal.[264] It was 'a quite different matter to suppose that [the general requirement of fairness in the admission of evidence in criminal proceedings] will in its application involve throughout the civilised world the same results as would follow in England from decided authorities, whether under s 78 of PACE or under common law'.

---

[260] At 991. [261] *R* v. *Whiteley* [2005] EWCA Crim 699 at [12]–[13].

[262] *R* v. *Bow Street Magistrates' Court, ex parte Proulx* [2001] 1 All ER 57 (QB).

[263] At [75]. [264] At [78]–[79].

Conclusion

It seems that the success of the Mr Big techniques will lead to their continuation, perhaps modified to avoid the risks identified by the Canadian Supreme Court in *Hart*. The Royal Canadian Mounted Police have already announced modifications to the design of the operations to meet the concerns expressed in *Hart*, particularly in relation to targeting suspects who are isolated or vulnerable, including by reason of youth.[265] The divisions in the courts which have considered the deception suggest, however, that the last word has not yet been written on these deceptions. Although not in the context of a Mr Big operation, some straws in the wind may be seen in the Court of Appeal's approval for the view taken in *Archbold* that a distinction is to be drawn between deceit which 'simply provides a defendant with an opportunity to confess' and 'trickery that positively induces a confession'.[266] It is suggested that only positive inducement is likely to result in a confession being excluded.[267] Whether this approach over

---

[265] See Daniel LeBlanc, 'RCMP to keep "Mr. Big" sting tactic', The Globe and Mail (online edn, 1 August 2014), available at: www.theglobeandmail.com (last accessed 9 November 2016); and Mike Cabana, 'RCMP statement following the Supreme Court of Canada decision in the *Nelson Hart* case' (Royal Canadian Mounted Police, 31 July 2014), available at: www.rcmp-grc.gc.ca (last accessed 9 November 2016).

[266] James Richardson, *Archbold: Criminal Pleading Evidence and Practice 2017* (65th edn, Sweet & Maxwell, London, 2016) at [15-581]; see *R* v. *Smurthwaite* [1994] 1 All ER 898 (CA); *R* v. *Christou* [1992] QB 979 (CA); and *R* v. *Shannon* [2001] 1 WLR 51 (CA).

[267] This approach adopts that familiar in entrapment cases: see *R* v. *Looseley* [2001] UKHL 53, [2001] 1 WLR 2060.

time will seem to conform sufficiently to the human rights to silence and to obtain legal advice remains to be seen. In the same way, the concept of 'active elicitation' relied upon by the Canadian Supreme Court in *Hebert* and by the New Zealand Supreme Court in *R* v. *Kumar* may need further consideration.[268] The position in Scotland seems to be more strict in the view that any active deception ('trap') will make a statement inadmissible.[269]

The divisions in final courts suggest that there is little agreement on the principles being applied when deceptive policing practices impact on the procedural rights to fair trial which are human rights. It seems time to get our thinking in order. Mr Big operations are simply the latest wave in developing investigative practices. If the right to silence and the associated right to legal advice exist to provide choice to a defendant as to whether he will speak or not, then tricks which result in confessions without that choice being

---

[268] *R* v. *Kumar* [2015] NZSC 124, [2016] 1 NZLR 204. In that case, the majority adopted a test of 'active elicitation' to determine whether the right to silence was breached. The 'key consideration' in that enquiry was 'whether the undercover officer directed the conversation in a way that "prompted, coaxed or cajoled" the suspect to make the statements': at [43]. The minority judgment did not agree that there must be a 'functional equivalent of interrogation' or direction by police in a manner that 'prompts, coaxes or cajoles'; that unduly elevated the causal connection required. Rather, 'active elicitation' was to be understood in contradistinction to passive observation: at [114]–[115].

[269] See *HM Advocate* v. *Higgins* [2006] SLT 946 where confessions obtained by passive listening were ruled inadmissible because the accused had been deliberately placed in adjacent cells and were tricked into thinking that they could not be overheard. See also *HM Advocate* v. *Campbell* 1964 JC 80.

provided undermine the substantive right. The result is irreparable by subsequent parade of fair process at trial, for the reasons identified by the European Court of Human Rights in *Salduz* and by the UK Supreme Court in *Cadder*. An admissible confession obtained without choice informed by access to legal advice denies the presumption of innocence and the right to silence. Kirby J pointed out in connection with the voluntariness of a confession that the right to speak or not is 'overborne' when 'tricks and deception' are successfully 'targeted directly at the suspect's fundamental legal right under our criminal justice system, namely to remain silent in the presence of police investigators'.[270]

In jurisdictions that identify the right to silence and the right to legal advice to exercise it as human rights, it is not necessary to go as far as to establish that the will of the suspect has been 'overborne' except in relation to the choice to speak. As was pointed out in *Hebert* by McLachlin J, it is enough to amount to breach of rights if the suspect is tricked out of the choice that was his right.[271] It is necessary to consider whether a purposive view of the observance of human rights leaves scope for the view that there is no breach where a suspect is not in custody or where an inducement or threat that influences choice is made by an undercover officer who is not known to the suspect to be a police officer. The short point made by Kirby J is that this is 'formulaic' thinking and that the evasion of rights

---

[270] *Tofilau* v. *The Queen* [2007] HCA 39, (2007) 231 CLR 396 at [204].

[271] See above at the text accompanying n. 219; and *R* v. *Hebert* [1990] 2 SCR 151 at 166–7.

constitutes breach in fact.[272] Even if a policy of the right is to protect those in custody because of their particular vulnerability, it is necessary to confront a point made by Lord Kerr in the UK Supreme Court in that '[t]here is no warrant for the belief that vulnerability descends at the moment that one is taken into custody and that it is absent until that vital moment'.[273] Those questioned by the police without legal advice may have little notion of the extent to which they are vulnerable.

It is also necessary to consider the impact of the deception in the particular case. In the case of enacted scenarios as elaborate as a Mr Big operation, it is not far-fetched to see the suspect as being under state control.[274] His apparent choice is manipulated by tricks mobilised by the superior resources and power of the state.[275] The deceptions impact upon dignity and rule of law values which underlie human rights. Because scenario operations designed to obtain confessions inevitably seek to provide incentives for confidences, they engage concerns about inducements and voluntariness, which have traditionally prompted caution at common law. The Mr Big interviews themselves raise red flags in terms of what is known to risk false confessions. Although it is suggested in some of the cases that concern should be reserved for those with special vulnerabilities only, it may come to be seen that the psychological pressures used in scenario

[272] *Tofilau* v. *The Queen* [2007] HCA 39, (2007) 231 CLR 396 at [188].
[273] *Ambrose* v. *Harris* [2011] UKSC 43, [2011] 1 WLR 2435 at [136].
[274] As argued by Adeline Iftene, 'The Hart of the (Mr.) Big problem' (2016) 63 *Crim LQ* 178 at 195.
[275] *R* v. *Hebert* [1990] 2 SCR 151 at 176.

operations themselves create vulnerabilities.[276] Deceptive practices by agents of the state also raise rule of law issues which should be weighed because the procedures of criminal justice are 'a check on the powers of the state and an important defence for individual liberty'.[277] Kirby J, in speaking of this consideration said, in terms with which I am sure Miss Hamlyn and Lord Denning would have agreed, that this is 'a reason why countries that observe the accusatorial system tend to have a higher quality of liberty than countries that observe different traditions'.[278]

I do not want to blow that trumpet. My point is that we need to work harder at the conceptual underpinnings of our system of criminal justice. That is a responsibility Miss Hamlyn thought to be one shared by all who benefit from British justice. In talking of the experience that safeguards are required in criminal justice to protect against the 'overzealous as well as the despotic', Felix Frankfurter said the procedural protections of law reflect not a sentimental but a sturdy view of law enforcement.[279] It was one that outlawed 'easy but self-defeating ways in which brutality is substituted for brains as an instrument of crime detection'.[280] The substitution of brains for brutality, however, brings its own challenges. If brains are not to be almost as self-defeating of

---

[276] See T. E. Moore, P. Copeland, and R. A. Schuller, 'Deceit, betrayal and the search for truth: legal and psychological perspectives on the "Mr. Big" strategy' (2010) 55 *Crim LQ* 348 at 381–2.

[277] *Carr* v. *Western Australia* [2007] HCA 47, (2007) 232 CLR 138 at [104].

[278] At [104].   [279] *McNabb* v. *United States* 318 US 332 (1943) at 343.

[280] At 344.

legitimacy as brutality, they need to be curbed by the rule of law. We should keep to the navigation lights provided by the fundamental principles now acknowledged to be human rights: the presumption of innocence and the right to silence.

Lecture 3

'The Most Important of All Judicial Functions'

In the first Lecture I discussed some of the features of British criminal justice in part by reference to the first trials conducted in New Zealand following the Treaty of Waitangi in 1840. The features included the linked principles of the presumption of innocence and the right to silence, looked at further in the second Lecture. In this, the final Lecture, I want to look at the institutional elements of the criminal justice system illustrated in those early New Zealand trials and the challenges they face today.

When 17-year-old Maketu Wharetotara was tried for murder in 1842 in the Supreme Court in Auckland, Chief Justice Martin was determined to demonstrate to Maori the virtues of British justice and its superiority over the pre-European system of kin responsibility. The trial was followed closely by the many Maori who attended the Court and discussed in the Maori language newspapers which circulated through the country. What most impressed them was the deliberation, 'calmness', and care in the process of proof in public before a judge and jury.[281] It helped, too, that there were two criminal trials held in the Supreme Court session.

[281] See W. Swainson, *New Zealand and its Colonisation* (Smith Elder, London, 1859) at 58–9; and William Martin, 'Observations on the proposal to take native lands under an Act of the Assembly' [1864] I *AJHR* E2c at 6.

The other was of a European who was charged with an assault on a Maori. So there was a demonstration of equal treatment under law. The different roles played by judge, prosecution, and defence counsel followed the accusatory mode of trial familiar still today, but then only recently established in English criminal procedure. The state, rather than the relatives of Maketu's victims, offered proof of guilt in a public forum for determination by a jury of twelve. The trial was under the control of a judge who was conspicuously detached from the fray and who applied principles and practices developed by the courts to ensure that what was 'fair and just' was done between prosecution and defence.[282]

A Sea Change?

For much of the intervening 170 years, these characteristics of the system have remained relatively constant. More recently, however, there has been considerable change, originally judge-led but now contained in enacted rules of criminal procedure.[283] The over-riding objective of the rules of procedure remains that criminal cases be dealt with justly. What is 'just' is now defined in the Criminal Procedure Rules here to include 'acquitting the innocent and convicting the guilty' and the efficient and expeditious conduct of cases in

---

[282] *Connelly* v. *Director of Public Prosecutions* [1964] AC 1254 (HL) at 1347–8 per Lord Devlin.

[283] Described by Thomas LJ, referring to the Criminal Procedure Rules 2005, as a 'sea change': *R (on the application of the Director of Public Prosecutions)* v. *Chorley Justices* [2006] EWHC 1795 (Admin), [2006] All ER (D) 55 at [24].

a manner that 'takes into account the gravity of the offence alleged, the complexity of what is in issue, the severity of the consequences for the defendant and others affected, and the needs of other cases'.[284] These objectives are imposed on all participants in the system, including the judge. In other common law jurisdictions there are comparable rules.[285]

The idea of proportionality in the treatment accorded criminal cases according to whether they are 'grave' or 'complex' and 'the needs of other cases' is something of a shift. The traditional view has been that any criminal conviction is always grave, both for the individual and for society. The reference to 'convicting the guilty' and 'acquitting the innocent' is also something of a change in focus from the view that the purpose of criminal justice is the sufficiency of proof of guilt. The traditional understanding was expressed by Baroness Hale:[286]

> Innocence as such is not a concept known to our criminal justice system. We distinguish between the guilty and the not guilty. A person is only guilty if the state can prove his guilt beyond reasonable doubt. This is, as Viscount Sankey

---

[284] Criminal Procedure Rules 2005, r 1.1(2).

[285] In New Zealand, the Criminal Procedure Rules 2012 seek to secure the 'just and timely determination of proceedings under the [Criminal Procedure] Act': r1.3(b). Section 55(1) of the Criminal Procedure Act 2011 similarly stresses the need for case management discussions between prosecution and defence 'to make arrangements necessary for its fair and expeditious resolution'. In Victoria, the Criminal Procedure Act 2009 (Vic), s 181 refers to the powers of the court at a direction hearing to ensure 'the fair and efficient conduct of proceedings'.

[286] *R (Adams)* v. *Secretary of State for Justice; In re MacDermott & McCartney* [2011] UKSC 18, [2012] 1 AC 48 at [116].

LC so famously put it in *Woolmington* v. *Director of Public Prosecutions* [1935] AC 462, 481, the 'golden thread' which is always to be seen 'throughout the web of the English criminal law'. Only then is the state entitled to punish him. Otherwise he is not guilty, irrespective of whether he is in fact innocent.

Nothing in the current rules suggests or could permit corner-cutting that would result in unfair trial or breach of fundamental rights. The rules are designed, as Lord Woolf said, to achieve a 'culture change in criminal case management' without affecting the right to a fair trial or detracting from the right to silence or legal privilege.[287] But there has been some nervousness nevertheless that the door has been opened to managerial and perhaps indignant judging, which was not the tradition of detachment which found approval in New Zealand in 1842.

In her 2008 Hamlyn Lectures, Dame Hazel Genn suggested that the civil justice reforms (themselves driven in part by the burgeoning costs of the criminal justice system) had 'fundamentally changed the nature of the judicial role' by requiring the judge to be an active case manager, balancing values of efficiency and cost-effectiveness, rather than a 'remote and passive umpire'.[288] She took the view that the method of case management against the objectives of efficiency and the promotion of deals and settlements treats

---

[287] Lord Woolf, 'The objectives and content of the first Criminal Procedure Rules', Ministry of Justice (March 2005).

[288] Hazel Genn, *Judging Civil Justice* (The Hamlyn Lectures, Cambridge University Press, 2010) at 173.

trial as system failure.[289] Genn's verdict was that, in a system where efficiency seems valued above substantively right outcomes, there are 'no rights that cannot be compromised and ... every conflict represents merely a clash of morally equivalent interests'.[290] I do not here enter into the debate about whether there are justifications for taking this road in civil justice. But similar effects can now be observed in criminal justice. In that context there are real questions about whether they can be reconciled with fundamental elements of the system.

Negotiated resolution, avoidance of public determination of guilt, focus on efficiency and cost, and administrative emphasis on measurable outputs are the conditions of criminal justice today. The public good in adjudication, the virtue Chief Justice Martin was so anxious to display in the first trial in New Zealand, does not seem as valued. Trial is seen by courts administrators as system failure. Emphasis on maximising use of courtroom facilities (in large part to dampen demand for more buildings) and the running down of support for the administration of criminal justice is resulting in pressure on all involved with the system, which many think has become unreasonable and dangerous to proper process. Greater centralisation and remote participation enabled by modern technology may reduce costs but often increases burdens on participants or raises concerns about the dignity

---

[289] *Ibid.* at 174–5, in which Dame Hazel cites J. Resnik, 'Trial as error, jurisdiction as injury: transforming the meaning of Article III' (2000) 113 *Harv L Rev* 924.

[290] *Ibid.* at 25.

of those being processed and about the public administration of justice.[291]

Court staff and judges are required to manage cases and ration procedure, and to pursue the goals of efficiency and expedition. Participants in the system speak of a dispiriting loss of morale, of upheavals and strains through constant change, of a culture of finger-pointing and some anger, and unintended consequences when modifications to achieve efficiencies at one stage cause consequential delays and additional effort at another stage of the process.[292] It is not even clear what the pain is achieving. The National Audit Office here has acknowledged the

[291] In some areas of New Zealand, for example, bail applications can be heard only in 'list courts'. In areas where a list court is held only on specific days of the week, there may be considerable travel required to get a bail application before a judge, and there are suggestions that defendants and their counsel may acquiesce in longer remands in custody than are warranted so that the matter can be called in the scheduled list day.

[292] Recent streamlining in New Zealand to provide for first call of criminal cases to be an 'administrative' hearing (usually before a registrar) has led to guilty pleas being deferred to the second, review, hearing (usually before a judge). The result of the change has been that instead of guilty pleas being entered at the first appearance, as was usual in the overwhelming proportion of cases under the old system, a high proportion of cases now go to the review hearing. It is not clear whether that result is partly a consequence of the ability to seek a pre-plea sentence indication at a review hearing or whether it is influenced in part by the strict timetabling requirements under the new regime. Similar effect was seen in England and Wales when committal hearings were abolished, transferring delays to the trial court from the Magistrates' Courts: see Comptroller and Auditor General, *Efficiency in the Criminal Justice System* (National Audit Office, HC 852, 1 March 2016) at [1.10].

difficulties in measuring the performance of the courts in a recent report on criminal justice: 'The system has a number of objectives, which can be in tension, and it is not possible to know for certain whether a case has produced the "right" result in terms of convicting all those who are guilty and no one who is innocent.'[293] The National Audit Office pointed out that a target rate for guilty pleas (a measurement monitored in most jurisdictions),[294] 'could discourage prosecution of hard-to-prosecute cases or encourage unreasonable pressure on defendants to plead guilty early'.[295] It observed that pressure on parts of the system to make financial savings may shift burdens unfairly.[296]

---

[293] *Ibid.* at [1.12].

[294] The National Audit Office's report acknowledged at [1.12] that the Ministry monitors rates of guilty pleas. Similarly, in New Zealand, rates of guilty pleas are monitored: see, for example, Geoffrey Venning, *Report from the High Court 2015 – the Year in Review* (17 May 2016) at 6.

[295] Comptroller and Auditor General, *Efficiency in the Criminal Justice System* (National Audit Office, HC 852, 1 March 2016) at [1.12]. The report recorded that the Ministry's primary measures of the effectiveness of the system are the proportion of cases that go ahead as scheduled and the time it takes for cases to progress through the system.

[296] *Ibid.* at [2.12]. The report observed that inadequate incentives exist for organisations to work together to achieve wider benefits. 'There are currently no incentives to encourage organisations to take the best course of action for the whole system. . . . Costs are therefore shunted from one part of the system to another, rather than being removed from the system altogether. For example, the police may choose not to request expensive forensic evidence to reduce their costs, but this can make it harder for the prosecution to prepare a strong case to persuade a defendant to plead guilty rather than go to court.'

What is Driving Criminal Justice?

What is driving criminal justice today is more significant than a shift in judicial attitudes and the introduction of modern methods of case management borrowed from the civil justice reforms. There seems also to have been a shift in community and political attitudes to public justice more generally and to criminal justice in particular. There may have been a backlash against processes which are seen to be too costly, too time-consuming, too tender of the interests of defendants, and too much of a gravy train for lawyers.[297] Anti-lawyer rhetoric has been a striking background feature of reforms to criminal justice in a number of jurisdictions.

Another background factor has been the politicisation of crime described by Professor Nicola Lacey in her Hamlyn Lectures. In a number of societies there has been lack of leadership in addressing the causes of crime and in allowing fear of crime to be talked up.[298] Lacey referred to the

---

[297] Such views may be behind legislative classifications of penalties or preventive orders as 'civil', a trend that the European Court of Human Rights has not been prepared to take at face value in considering whether rights of criminal process are implicated: *Benham* v. *United Kingdom* (1996) 22 EHRR 293 (ECHR) at [56]; and *Engel* v. *Netherlands* (1979) 1 EHRR 647 (ECHR) at [81]–[85]. This approach has been endorsed more recently. In *Ezeh and Connors* v. *United Kingdom* (2004) 39 EHRR 1 (ECHR), which concerned the imposition of punishments on prisoners for ill-discipline in prison, the Court found these were criminal for the purposes of the Convention.

[298] During much of the period during which crime has emerged as a significant political issue, crime rates have in fact been falling. To some extent that is a consequence of the ageing population: Sonja Dekker and John Bryant, 'Ageing and violent crimes in New Zealand' (Statistics

opening this had provided to 'well-organised single-issue pressure groups, notably those representing the interest of victims of crime' which have had an impact on the shape of criminal justice today.[299]

One of the more significant changes in criminal justice in recent years has been its repositioning around the victim.[300] That focus has inevitably affected public ownership of criminal justice, emphasised as a virtue of British criminal justice at Maketu's trial in New Zealand in 1842. David Garland has described the reintroduction of the victim as a participant as a 're-personalisation' of criminal justice.[301] That re-personalisation is not always an easy fit with processes designed, as Neil MacCormick and David Garland once put it, to 'turn hot vengeance into cool,

New Zealand Working Paper 10–01, September 2010). There are recent indications that some kinds of violent crime may be increasing. New Zealand recorded an increase in violent crime in the home and violent crime is increasing as a proportion of total offending: in its 2015–16 Annual Report, the New Zealand Ministry of Justice reported that while total crime had reduced by 15 per cent, violent crime had reduced by 4 per cent and therefore comprised a greater proportion of overall offending: Ministry of Justice *Annual Report* (1 July 2015–30 June 2016) at 17.

[299] Nicola Lacey, *The Prisoners' Dilemma: Political Economy and Punishment in Contemporary Democracies* (The Hamlyn Lectures, Cambridge University Press, 2008) at 68.

[300] *Ibid.* 68–70. In New Zealand, the victim has been said to be 'at the heart of decision making' within the justice sector: Hon. Amy Adams, 'Introduction from Minister of Justice' *Statement of Intent 2015–2019* (Ministry of Justice, Wellington, 2015) at 4.

[301] David Garland, 'The cultural uses of capital punishment' (2002) 4 *Punishment & Society* 459 at 464–5.

impartial justice'.[302] Courtrooms can now be angry places. The attempt to meet different interests adds to the complexities of managing hearings.[303] In addition, alternative methods of dealing with offending have been developed in part to further the aims of restorative justice and reparation and better meet the needs of victims.

There are a number of questions which may not have been adequately addressed in these changes. The most important is whether victims are indeed helped by being kept in thrall to the criminal justice processes. Concerns about re-victimisation or marginalisation in these processes are not uncommon, even in relation to alternative methods of resolution designed in part to meet the interests of victims.[304] That

[302] Neil MacCormick and David Garland, 'Sovereign states and vengeful victims: the problem of the right to punish' in Andrew Ashworth and Martin Wasik (eds.) *Fundamentals of Sentencing Theory: Essays in Honour of Andrew von Hirsch* (Clarendon Press, Oxford, 1998) 11 at 26.

[303] That is not only in managing the dynamics at trial but in accommodating preferences in scheduling hearings (victims in New Zealand have the right to be present at every court event). Victims must be provided with information about the date and place of each court event (see Victims' Rights Act 2002, s 12(2)); and victims or their representatives are entitled to attend the Family Group Conference, a restorative justice forum, and Youth Court proceedings (see Children, Young Persons and Their Families Act 1989, ss 251(f) and 329(ja)).

[304] In New Zealand, the Independent Police Conduct Authority released a report on the use of pre-charge warnings following complaint from a police officer. One of the bases for his complaint was that the system of pre-charge warnings undermined victims' rights, because it took insufficient consideration of victims' views and denied victims the chance to seek reparation for financial loss (see Independent Police Conduct Authority, *Review of Pre-charge Warnings* (14 September 2016, Wellington) at [2]–[7]). In the review of out-of-court disposals in 2015,

may be inevitable. If equality of treatment is important to criminal justice, there are limits to the extent to which procedures and outcomes can turn on the different preferences of individual victims without compromising basic principles about equality before the law. There is no question of going back to the days when victims were largely irrelevant and were not well treated as witnesses. But it would be good, before we load any more into the criminal justice system, to understand whether there are better responses to be made for victims than within the system of proof of guilt and punishment of offenders.

The criminal justice system today has also been affected by changes to government administration. The new public management model treats the wider criminal justice sector as an integrated system. Reducing cost, and in particular the cost of prisons, is a substantial focus of this joined-up model of government. So too is sharing information. In New Zealand, the sector is referred to openly by the Ministry of Justice as a 'pipeline'.[305] A purpose of the pipeline

a House of Commons Committee recommended greater involvement by victims in scrutiny panels, which are responsible for overseeing the use of out-of-court disposals: House of Commons Home Affairs Committee, 'Out-of-court disposals' (Fourteenth Report of Session 2014–2015, The Stationery Office, London, 2015) at [34]–[35].

[305] The 'pipeline' was explained by the Ministry of Justice as follows: 'We can think about the criminal justice system (Police, Justice/Courts and Corrections) as a "pipeline". The pipeline starts with Police preventing and dealing with crime, moves through to the Courts where offenders are prosecuted and sentenced, and ends with Corrections who manage prison and community sentences, and provide rehabilitation programmes. It means policies and approaches in one part of the system

model is to allow better management across the sector to alleviate pressures where they arise and to achieve government targets, including the reduction of crime and the demand for prison beds.[306] Modern technology is seen as providing opportunities to reduce costs and achieve better timeliness and better cooperation between public agencies. These trends will be familiar to all because it is clear that administrators in different jurisdictions keep in touch and copy each other.

There may be very good administrative sense in these methods. But it means that the courts in the middle of the pipeline are not seen as standing apart from the whole of

can impact on others. Joining up our approach allows us to identify these effects, and implement changes that have the best outcomes for everyone': Ministry of Justice, 'About the justice sector' (updated 1 November 2016), available at: www.justice.govt.nz (last accessed 8 November 2016). So, for example, one aim in a proposed sentencing reform (not implemented in the end) was explained as intended to give the executive 'significantly enhanced control of its Corrections budget': Law Commission, *Sentencing Guidelines and Parole Reform* (NZLC R94, 2006) at [74]; and to help correct 'a disconnect between supply and demand [for prison beds] that would not be regarded as acceptable in other areas of public expenditure': Law Commission, *Reforms to the Sentencing and Parole Structure: Consultation Draft* (NZLC PP0, 2006) at [3].

[306] In New Zealand, the Ministry of Justice action plan of targets to be achieved by 2017 includes reducing the overall crime rate by 15 per cent, reducing violent crime by 20 per cent, reducing the youth crime rate by 5 per cent, and reducing re-offending by 25 per cent (starting from a base as of June 2011): Ministry of Justice, 'Delivering better public services: reducing crime and re-offending – result action plan' (July 2012), available at: www.justice.govt.nz (last accessed 11 November 2016).

government effort.[307] In New Zealand, the Ministry of Justice, which supports the courts, is the lead agency in a justice sector which includes the police, Crown prosecutors, and the Department of Corrections. Within the Ministry of Justice itself are located not only the administration of courts and tribunals but the administration of legal aid[308] and the Public Defence Service (a new service which is intended to provide legal representation in approximately 50 per cent of criminal legal aid cases).[309] It is easy to see that with such broad responsibilities the narrower values of the criminal justice system applied in the courts are not the focus and can be overlooked. Registrars and sometimes judges are reported to put pressure on counsel to advance or resolve cases within time frames that may not be appropriate to meet the evidential and other issues thrown up by the particular case, because of general Ministry goals such as that 'all serious harm cases [will be] disposed of within 12 months'.[310]

[307] A recent example is provided by Ministry of Justice officials arranging administratively with registry officers to give priority in scheduling of cases at the request of Corrections to alleviate a shortage of custodial beds for women on remand.

[308] The former independent Legal Service Agency having been brought into the Ministry: see Hon. Simon Power, 'Changes at Legal Services Agency' (press release, 30 November 2009), available at: www.beehive.govt.nz (last accessed 11 November 2016).

[309] Hon. Simon Power, 'Minister welcomes opening of Hamilton Public Defence Service' (press release, 1 June 2011), available at: www.beehive.govt.nz (last accessed 11 November 2016).

[310] Ministry of Justice *Annual Report* (1 July 2015–30 June 2016) at 10, available at: www.justice.govt.nz (last accessed 11 November 2016). An informal goal in the High Court of nine months from first appearance to trial has been abandoned after demonstration that the

Criminal Justice Out of Sight

Much criminal justice is today undertaken outside the public view. That has always been true of the early stages of criminal process because of police and prosecutorial charging discretions, which the courts have traditionally been reluctant to supervise.[311] But today there is more systematic and extensive management of offending away from the courts. It is a development which has been undertaken by administrative measures in large part rather than by legislative reform.

Lord Judge, when Lord Chief Justice, voiced concern about the extent of out-of-court disposals, particularly through the use of police warnings and cautions, and their potential to affect public confidence in criminal justice institutions.[312] He stressed that this was not a question of

time was insufficient for the briefing of police witnesses and the obtaining of reports.

[311] In *Gill* v. *Attorney-General* [2010] NZCA 468, [2011] 1 NZLR 433 the Court of Appeal said at [19]: 'the courts have held that they will only intervene in matters which involve the exercise of a prosecutorial discretion or investigative power in exceptional cases'. See also *Fox* v. *Attorney-General* [2002] 3 NZLR 62 (CA) at [28]–[31] and the cases cited therein. There it was noted that courts' reluctance to interfere with decisions to initiate and continue prosecution 'reflects constitutional sensitivities in light of the Courts' own function of responsibility for conduct of criminal trials'. Variations in practice in the exercise of charging discretions were one of the reasons that led Auld LJ to make recommendations for better oversight of charging through the Crown Prosecution Service: see Lord Justice Auld, *Review of the Criminal Courts of England and Wales* (HM Stationery Office, September 2001) at [10.38].

[312] Lord Judge, '*Summary justice in and out of court*' (John Harris Memorial Lecture, Drapers Hall, London, 7 July 2011) at 17.

'turf wars' between courts and police. Rather, it was about 'the public interest in the open and transparent administration of justice'. Lord Judge referred to the risk of creating a parallel justice system in which police officers act as prosecutor, jury, and judge.[313] Similarly, Lord Justice Leveson has pointed to the erosion of important values of open justice through the scale of out of court resolution of cases and the significant consequences for those who may mistakenly think that they are easy and soft options.[314] Although, following these expressions of concern, the number of out-of-court disposals in England and Wales has reduced from a peak in 2008, the use of warnings and cautions remains high.[315]

In New Zealand, 40 per cent of police apprehensions now are dealt with by alternative processes which do not lead to prosecution.[316] In addition to informal police warnings, cases

---

[313] *Ibid.* at 15.

[314] In 2010, Lord Justice Leveson raised concerns about the number of offences being resolved outside the courtroom: '*Criminal justice in the 21st century*' (The Roscoe Lecture, St George's Hall, Liverpool, 29 November 2010). He raised questions about the scale of methods of disposal of criminal proceedings and the fact that the police acted essentially as both prosecutor and judge, without supervision. He questioned the erosion of the system of public justice conducted by magistrates.

[315] See Ministry of Justice, 'Putting an end to "soft option" cautions' (press release, 1 November 2014), available at: www.gov.uk (last accessed 18 November 2016). A pilot programme aimed at simplifying the system of out-of-court disposals has been under way since late 2014 and may be expected to lead to further changes.

[316] The proportion of police apprehensions that ended in a prosecution was 60 per cent in 2011, compared with about 70 per cent in 2006–9. Apprehensions ending in prosecution were 63 per cent in 2014,

can be the subject of formal diversion. Diversion was originally available only for first offenders, but that requirement has been relaxed.[317] It is not a legislative process, although there is some recognition of diversion in legislation in that registrars or the court are given a power by legislation to dismiss charges once the police prosecutor advises that an agreed programme of diversion has been completed.[318] In the last ten years, the New Zealand Police have also introduced a system of formal police warnings patterned on the police warning system in England and Wales discussed by Lord Judge and Lord Justice Leveson.[319] Because of the police warning system, the number of diversions has diminished, as have discharges without conviction (a judge-imposed statutory resolution).[320]

---

59 per cent in 2013, and 58 per cent in 2012. The raw data is available at Statistics New Zealand, 'New Zealand recorded crime tables' (2015), available at: www.stats.govt.nz (last accessed 11 November 2016).
The number of adults charged in court in 2015 was the lowest since the series of records began in 1980: see Ministry of Justice, 'Trends in conviction and sentencing in New Zealand' (2015), available at: www.justice.govt.nz (last accessed 11 November 2016).

[317] This occurred in 2013.

[318] The only legislative acknowledgement of the process of diversion is the power to dismiss the charge on proof that a programme of diversion has been completed: see Criminal Procedure Act 2011, s 148.

[319] The system was introduced in New Zealand in 2009 for offences carrying a maximum penalty of six months' imprisonment. An original target that 9 per cent of arrests would be dealt with by pre-charge warnings has been exceeded: see New Zealand Police, 'Policing excellence update' (7 September 2012); as cited in Mark O'Regan, 'Criminal justice institutions in times of change' (13th International Criminal Law Congress, Queenstown, New Zealand, 12–16 September 2012) at 6.

[320] From 2009 to 2015 there has been a decline by about a third in the rate of discharges without conviction and diversion. A decline in the

As a result, much offending has moved out of the supervision of the courts altogether. Diversion has now been extended to cover offending carrying a maximum penalty of more than six months' imprisonment.[321] Both diversion and pre-charge warnings are subject to police guidelines. Both often incorporate elements of restorative justice programmes and reparation. Both require written admission of guilt, although no formal plea is required in the court and the

proportion of charges prosecuted against adults that resulted in diversion or discharge without conviction is shown in the information available at Statistics New Zealand, 'New Zealand recorded crime tables' (2015), available at: www.stats.govt.nz (last accessed 11 November 2016). While there is no statutory basis for the diversion scheme – it is a restorative justice initiative of the police – it is recognised in statute: see above at n. 318. A decision to discharge without conviction is made by a judge: Sentencing Act 2002, ss 106–7. A discharge without conviction cannot occur 'unless the court is satisfied that the direct and indirect consequences of a conviction would be out of all proportion to the gravity of the offence'.

[321] A number of police officers explained to the Independent Police Conduct Authority that 'the introduction of pre-charge warnings means that diversion is generally now used for offences with a maximum penalty of more than six months' imprisonment'. The review considered that, if that is the intent, it should be made clear in policy documents: Independent Police Conduct Authority, *Review of Pre-charge Warnings* (14 September 2016, Wellington) at [124]. For a defendant to receive diversion, he or she must enter into a written acknowledgement of responsibility and conditions, including any reparation or counselling or agreement to undertake a restorative justice programme. Once the conditions are fulfilled, the police prosecutor advises the court and the defendant is not required to attend the court again. Withdrawal of the charges is made by a registrar or the court on the prosecutor's application. See New Zealand Police, 'About the adult diversion scheme', available at: www.police.govt.nz (last accessed 9 November 2016).

charges are delayed or adjourned and later withdrawn to allow the alternative procedures to be put in place (in the case of diversion after fulfilment of any required programme). Although the supervision exercised by the court over diversion is slight, there is no court oversight at all over pre-charge warnings.[322]

A recent report by the Independent Police Conduct Authority in New Zealand has found inconsistency in use of pre-charge warnings and disparity in the treatment of Maori and non-Maori.[323] The Authority found varying practices in relation to consultation with victims and the extent to which previous criminal history was disqualifying. It found there was a lack of integration with the other alternative actions of informal warnings and diversion. Informal warnings were, perversely, often given in respect of offending too serious to receive a pre-

---

[322] The fact that a pre-charge warning has been given is information that is retained and may be used in subsequent proceedings. The offender must admit the offence. Victim considerations must be taken into account but a pre-charge warning is not contingent on the victim agreeing to such course. Reparations must be taken into account but a pre-charge warning is not dependent on reparation having been paid. Criminal history and previous pre-charge warnings must be taken into account but there is no prohibition on second or subsequent pre-charge warnings being issued. See Independent Police Conduct Authority, *Review of Pre-charge Warnings* (14 September 2016, Wellington) at 4–5.

[323] Although the Authority declined to draw the conclusion that the differential treatment was based on ethnicity, it was troubled by the disparity and suggested more guidance. Independent Police Conduct Authority, *Review of Pre-charge Warnings* (14 September 2016, Wellington) at [76]–[84].

charge warning.[324] Pre-charge warnings were sometimes given to those who were not eligible for diversion under the guidelines.[325] The Independent Police Conduct Authority found inadequate recording and inadequate observance of guidelines as to the seriousness of offences.[326]

Similar lack of consistency has been identified in the comparable out-of-court police warning system in England and Wales. Reports in 2011 and 2015 have found non-compliance with guidelines and significant regional variations in application.[327] As is the case in New Zealand, the recording of warnings was unsatisfactory and meant that previous warnings were sometimes overlooked. There was lack of clarity about the circumstances in which alternative methods

---

[324] *Ibid.* at [119]–[121].

[325] The Authority considered it was unclear whether recidivist offenders could be offered diversion to ensure payment of reparation. Some offenders received a pre-charge warning where they may not have been eligible for diversion due to previous convictions (even following the 2013 change to expand diversion beyond first-time offenders): see Independent Police Conduct Authority, *Review of Pre-charge Warnings* (14 September 2016, Wellington) at [122]–[126].

[326] *Ibid.* at [120]–[121] and [127]–[130].

[327] See Criminal Justice Joint Inspection, 'Exercising discretion: the gateway to justice' (June 2011), available at: www.hmic.gov.uk (last accessed 10 October 2016). In 2015, the House of Commons Home Affairs Committee found that between 20 and 33 per cent of out-of-court disposals had been dealt with inappropriately: House of Commons Home Affairs Committee, 'Out-of-court disposals' (14th Report of the Session 2014–2015, The Stationery Office, 6 March 2015) at 2.

of dealing with offenders were used instead of out-of-court warnings.[328]

Police warnings and police diversion are not the only way in which cases are being resolved outside the courts. In England and Wales and in New Zealand, some offenders are dealt with by neighbourhood or community justice panels. In New Zealand, this is under a pilot programme in one city. There is no statutory underpinning for the process. Removal at the option of the police to community or neighbourhood panels is used in the case of offending where warnings are thought not to be a sufficient response.[329] The cases are said to be at 'the upper-level of offences that can be resolved without charge and prosecution'.[330] The review of the pilot indicates that some relatively serious offending has been referred, including a small number of family violence cases, as well as other offending generally thought to require charge before restorative justice is attempted.[331] It is not clear how decisions to refer to community panels have been taken

---

[328] *Ibid.* at [37].

[329] Lord Judge expressed misgivings about the use of such panels in his 2011 speech, in case they set up a third distinctive and separate method for the administration of summary justice: see Lord Judge, 'Summary justice in and out of Court' (John Harris Memorial Lecture, Drapers Hall, London, 7 July 2011) at 17–18, available at: www.judiciary.gov.uk (last accessed 10 October 2016).

[330] New Zealand Police, *Community Justice Panel in Christchurch: An Evaluation* (Alternative Resolutions Workstream, November 2012) at 2.

[331] Offences included burglary, assault on a child, and common and domestic assault. See the police's evaluation of the Christchurch pilot: *ibid.* at 11.

in such cases.[332] The panel pilot scheme is reported to have been successful. Only about 20 per cent of those referred are returned to be dealt with through the courts.[333] There are plans to expand panels in partnership with local iwi (tribes) in particular areas.[334] An experienced New Zealand judge has described the panels as an alternative justice system without the protections and without the trained participants.[335] Indeed, one of the project's developers said '[w]e don't see ourselves as

---

[332] The evaluation of the pilot indicated that the team leading the pilot considered there was an opportunity 'to test the approach on a broader range of offences, to see if the eligibility criteria could be expanded'. The pilot was there expanded to lower-level offences of violence (which were not eligible for a police warning). The aim was to see whether 'greater victim involvement and a process to identify underlying drivers of crime could achieve more effective resolutions in these cases'. It was reported that further consultation indicated that in cases of family violence (which seem to have been those used in the extension) the police view was that alternative resolutions for family violence should only be initiated after charges had been laid and not through the pre-charge community panel process. See New Zealand Police, *Community Justice Panel in Christchurch: An Evaluation* (Alternative Resolutions Workstream, November 2012) at 11 and 46.

[333] *Ibid.* at 33.

[334] See Shaun Akroyd and others, *Iwi Panels: an Evaluation of their Implementation and Operation at Hutt Valley, Gisbourne, and Manukau from 2014 to 2015* (prepared for the Ministry of Justice, 17 June 2016) at 28; and Ministry of Justice, *Justice Matters* (Issue 3, June 2016) at 9, where the Ministry recorded that it is working with police 'to enhance the panels through police and strengthen iwi panel processes through a range of operational improvements'.

[335] He expressed concern about vetting and training, the pressure on defendants to accept the process, and the lack of distinction between investigative, prosecutorial, defence, and judicial functions. See Ronald Young, 'Has New Zealand's criminal justice system been

a legal process. We may have lawyers involved, but in their capacity as community members. We want to avoid the comparison with the courts and wider legal system.'[336]

Further removals from the ordinary courts may be on the cards. Proposals currently being considered in New Zealand for dealing with those accused of offences of sexual violence build on some of the elements of diversion but extend them to much more serious offending. They would apply at the option of the complainant to remove such cases from the criminal justice system.[337] These proposals, put forward by the New Zealand Law Commission, are similar to a Canadian model, which applies, however, only in exceptional circumstances approved by the Public Prosecutor.[338]

compromised?' (Harkness Henry Lecture, University of Waikato, 7 September 2016).

[336] James Greenland, 'Police to make decision about Community Justice Panels' (2 November 2015, New Zealand Law Society), available at: www .lawsociety.org.nz (last accessed 11 November 2016). At present the scheme has not been expanded beyond the pilot location. A Ministry of Justice spokesperson said '[a]ny future expansion ... will need to be carefully considered by justice sector leadership in terms of their benefits, effectiveness and "fit" within the wider justice system'.

[337] See Law Commission, *The Justice Response to Victims of Sexual Violence* (NZLC R136, 2015).

[338] The Canadian Criminal Code has provision for a form of restorative justice called 'alternative measures': see Criminal Code Canada RSC 1985 c C-46, s 717. If certain criteria are met, including acceptance of responsibility, a perpetrator may be referred to an alternative measures programme. Acceptance of responsibility cannot be used as evidence in future criminal proceedings. Although use of an alternative measure is not itself a bar to future proceedings, charges that have been laid must be dismissed if the perpetrator has totally complied with the conditions imposed. Alternative measures will usually not occur in cases of sexual offending because referral

No decision as to whether to implement the recommendations has been taken yet in New Zealand.[339] Under the proposals, complainants and defendants would undertake programmes to address the harm caused and facilitate an agreed resolution. Successful completion of the programme would result in a statutory bar against future prosecution for the particular matter.[340] These suggestions are put forward to meet the undoubted challenges in dealing with crimes of sexual violence without re-victimising complainants and the massive under-reporting of such crimes. I do not underestimate the extent of the problem or wish to criticise attempts to

must be in the interests of society and the victim. In British Columbia, alternative measures can be used for cases of sexual violence if there is special approval from the Regional or Deputy Regional Crown Counsel. However, '[s]uch approvals may be granted only where exceptional circumstances exist so that the use of alternative mechanisms is not inconsistent with the protection of society'. See Law Commission, *The Justice Response to Victims of Sexual Violence* (NZLC R136, 2015) Appendix B at [19]–[21].

[339] The proposal is presently under further consideration by the government: see Law Commission, *Government Response to the Law Commission report on 'The Justice Response to Victims of Sexual Violence: Criminal Trials and Alternative Processes'* (Presented to the House of Representatives), available at: www.lawcom.govt.nz (last accessed 18 November 2016).

[340] The proposals were not without controversy – indeed an earlier proposal to adopt for the prosecution of sexual offending a more inquisitorial model without a jury was initially scuttled by a Minister concerned about the shift away from adversarialism: see Isaac Davison, 'Collins rules out changes to trials for child, sex victims' *New Zealand Herald* (online edn, 24 September 2012). Another concern was that victims will be pressured to opt for the alternative model to prosecution if police or the prosecutor considers the chance of bringing a successful prosecution to be low.

address it, but the proposals have the potential to undermine the principle of public justice and to open the door to unequal application of the criminal law in cases of serious offending, according to the attitude of the complainant or, perhaps, the complainant's family.

Pre-charge warnings, and the resolution of cases through community justice panels, have consequences for those who are dealt with under them. Offending must be admitted. Although the actual offence cannot be prosecuted once there is resolution, the admission forms part of the police record and is maintained as part of the person's 'criminal history'. The person receiving a pre-charge warning is required to sign a statement acknowledging that 'a record of this warning will be held by Police and may be used to determine your eligibility for any subsequent warnings, and may also be presented to the court during any future court proceedings'.[341] The information obtained through these processes, including the acknowledgement of guilt, is also information which may be shared by the police with other agencies and can be used in the police vetting increasingly resorted to by public and private bodies.[342] The acknowledgement of guilt

---

[341] A copy of the 'Pre-Charge Warning and Release Note' used in the Auckland pilot is available in Justine O'Reilly, *New Zealand Police Pre-Charge Warnings Alternative Resolutions: Evaluation Report* (Wellington, December 2010) at Appendix 13. A similar written acknowledgement is also required by persons receiving police cautions in England and Wales: see Ministry of Justice, *Code of Practice for Adult Conditional Cautions* (Stationery Office, London, January 2013) at [82].

[342] See New Zealand Police, 'Information about vetting', available at: www.police.govt.nz (last accessed 18 November 2016).

is also evidence that may be led as propensity evidence in respect of subsequent offending. These are therefore significant public law powers which potentially provide opportunities for intrusive social control of the individuals affected. There is a risk of over-criminalisation if people are incentivised into acquiescing in alternative resolution because it seems comparatively costless at the time.

It remains to be seen to what extent the courts will be drawn into supervising the use of these public powers. The suggestion that processes such as these are not part of the 'wider legal system' and stand apart from it is flawed. These processes impact on the protections of human rights and the procedural protections of fair criminal process. There are issues about access to legal advice before acquiescence in the process and exercise of the choice implicit in the right to silence. It is difficult to escape the feeling that some of these apparently ad hoc developments may not have been thought through in terms of fundamental principles such as the impact on the presumption of innocence, the right to silence, and the right to legal advice. The acknowledgements of responsibility are waivers of the right to silence and the presumption of innocence given in circumstances which may not provide proper opportunity for legal advice and informed choice.

The restorative justice and rehabilitative ends these processes permit also set up conditions of inequality in application of justice because they are not programmes universally available. Even those who are supportive of the goals of restorative justice and rehabilitative courts express concern that those who do not have access to such programmes are disadvantaged by geography or by the attitude of the particular victim. Although in sentencing in New Zealand judges must consider restorative justice outcomes,[343] the availability of access to such programmes is in practice limited by financial and practical considerations. The use of 'pilot' programmes in particular areas without attempt to set up universal access is inevitably discriminatory.

We should be very cautious about going down a path which relies heavily on law enforcement agencies to decide the laws they enforce and the manner of enforcement. Making substantive criminal responsibility depend on police or complainant procedural choice is a fundamental change in the direction taken by criminal justice in the last 200 years. Edward Gibbon described discretion about what amounts to crime as 'the first engine of tyranny'.[344] It is also a fundamental departure from equality before the law if criminal justice outcomes depend on access to programmes which are available to some only, without any rational basis for distinction. William Stuntz, in his sobering book *The Collapse of American Criminal Justice*, referred to criminal justice in the United States as a 'disorderly legal order, and a discriminatory one' where justice is dispensed not according to law but according to official discretion.[345] He raises concerns about the legitimacy of such a system and points to scholarship that

---

[343] Sentencing Act 2002, s 8(j) and 10.

[344] Edward Gibbon, *The History of the Decline and Fall of the Roman Empire* (Robinson, London, 1830) at 779.

[345] William Stuntz, *The Collapse of American Criminal Justice* (Harvard University Press, Cambridge Mass., 2011) at 4.

suggests that perceptions of illegitimacy themselves raise crime rates and exacerbate the difficulty of its control. He suggests closer attention to the fundamental value of equality before the law and more public determination of guilt, including through trial by jury. He expresses concerns about 'assembly line adjudication' (in which 'quick and casual' investigation and inadequate representation leads to 'equally quick and casual plea bargain between lawyers').[346]

I do not suggest that our criminal justice systems are in comparable crisis to that in the United States. But it is deeply worrying if the early reports on the new system of police warnings are showing indications in England and Wales and New Zealand of unequal treatment and discrimination. The criminal justice system cannot afford such taint. It shakes confidence in the system. The controversies that arise from time to time in any system if it is thought that particular offenders have received special treatment in the courts indicate that people in our societies care about equal treatment under law. They are reminders that instrumentalist aims for criminal justice may not meet community expectations and may be destructive of confidence in the system. Those controversies have arisen in cases which have taken place in courts, in public. It is not to be expected that there will be indifference to unequal treatment through the alternative ways in which criminal justice is managed today out of public sight.

[346] *Ibid.* at 57–8.

Encouragements to Plead

Cases that are not diverted from the criminal justice system or are not withdrawn have to be resolved formally by plea of guilty or by determination of guilt following proof. Only a tiny proportion of cases go to trial. And in all systems it is recognised that there are considerable savings in time and cost if guilty pleas are entered at an early stage. It is under-standable then that early pleas of guilty are encouraged. But care is needed because a guilty plea waives the fair trial rights against self-incrimination and to determination of guilt.[347]

Considerable inducements exist to plead guilty through the substantial discounting of sentences for guilty pleas now available through legislation and court decisions. The availability and ultimate effect of discounts is subject to discretionary judgements as to variables such as the time from which maximum discounts begin to diminish and whether or not to impose minimum non-parole periods.[348] The common

---

[347] In a submission on discounts for guilty pleas, the non-governmental organisation Fair Trials pointed out that the European Court of Human Rights 'has repeatedly held that any waiver of Convention rights "must be established in an unequivocal manner and must be attended by minimum safeguards commensurate with the waiver's importance." Furthermore, Courts must examine waivers of fair trial rights to see whether the circumstances surrounding the waiver were compatible with the requirements of the Convention, which should include an analysis of whether the waiver was given "knowingly and intelligently"': Fair Trials, 'Submission: reduction in sentence for a guilty plea guideline consultation' (London, May 2016) at [5] (citations omitted).

[348] Although guidelines on sentence discounts for guilty pleas proposed by the Sentencing Council would reduce judicial discretion in cases where the prosecution case is strong: see below at n. 354.

law has traditionally regarded admissions of guilt with suspicion when made under inducements. Just as is the case with confessions made to the police, guilty pleas may be false. They may be entered into because of a calculation of risk or simply to put an end to uncertainty, rather than because a guilty plea is right.[349] Guilty pleas which are known to be incorrect may arise more frequently in relatively trivial cases where the costs and vexation of pleading not guilty make it seem unworthwhile. We should not be complacent about admissions of guilt in those circumstances. But there is also reason to believe that the inducements to get matters resolved at a cost that is less than may be risked by post-trial sentence apply also to more serious offending. In a case in

---

[349] A study of the Crown Court carried out as part of the Runciman Commission on Criminal Justice found that 11 per cent of surveyed defendants who had pleaded guilty maintained their innocence: *The Royal Commission on Criminal Justice Crown Court Study* (Research Study No 19, HM Stationery Office, 1993) at 83. For more recent examples from the United Kingdom and Canada, see Penny Darbyshire, 'The mischief of plea bargaining and sentencing rewards' [2000] *Crim LR* 895 at 902–4; Joan Brockman, 'An offer you can't refuse: pleading guilty when innocent' (2010) *CLQ* 116 at 119–22; and Christopher Sherrin, 'Guilty pleas from the innocent' (2011) 30 *Windsor Rev Legal & Soc Issues* 1 at 3–7. See also *North Carolina v. Alford* 400 US 25 (1970), discussed below at n. 350; and *R v. Lawrence* [2013] EWCA Crim 1054, [2014] 1 WLR 106, discussed below at n. 352. In Western Australia, guidelines provide that a guilty plea will not be accepted if 'the accused person intimates that he or she is not guilty of any offence', indicating that the problem is common enough to require guidance for a judge: Director of Public Prosecutions for Western Australia, *Statement of Prosecution Policy and Guidelines* (2005) at [76](b).

the United States Supreme Court, the defendant pleaded guilty to murder despite maintaining his innocence because he did not want to be in jeopardy of the death penalty.[350] There are very high stakes indeed when alternatives available according to whether a plea is entered as soon as possible or at a late stage are apart by a number of years' imprisonment or where a minimum non-parole period hangs in the balance. These are powerful incentives to take the discount in very serious cases.

In the absence of effective legal advice the defendant may not appreciate that he is not guilty in law of the offence charged, particularly if he feels some responsibility for what has happened. The problem may be most acute in the case of an unrepresented defendant.[351] It would, however, be

---

[350] *North Carolina* v. *Alford* 400 US 25 (1970). The 'Alford plea', where a person pleads guilty to a crime they do not acknowledge committing, continues to be permitted in the United States. One article recorded that 47 states permit *Alford* pleas: see Stephanos Bibas, 'Harmonizing substantive-criminal-law values and criminal procedure: the case of Alford and nolo contendere pleas' (2003) 88 *Corn L Rev* 1361 at 1372, as cited by John H. Blume and Rebecca K. Helm, 'The unexonerated: factually innocent defendants who plead guilty' (2014) *Cornell Law Faculty Working Papers* 113 at 20. There are restrictions on acceptance of such pleas. In federal cases if the defendant maintains his or her innocence, federal attorneys must seek approval from an Assistant Attorney-General before entering a plea agreement, and must make an offer of proof of all facts known to the government to support the conclusion that the defendant is in fact guilty: see *United States Attorney's Manual: Title 9* at [9–27.440].

[351] One report noted there are no official figures for the number of unrepresented defendants in the magistrates' courts, though all interviewees in that study felt numbers had recently increased. It was

a mistake to think that represented litigants may not also enter incorrect pleas on inadequate legal advice. The Divisional Court, in allowing an appeal against a guilty plea which had been entered when the facts did not comprise the offence charged, recently called for more careful checking in relation to the 'streamlined' procedures directed at

suggested that in practice defendants typically will not be entitled to legal aid in the magistrates' court if they are accused of a non-imprisonable offence: Transform Justice, *Justice Denied? The Experience of Unrepresented Defendants in the Criminal Courts* (April 2016) at 2 and 6. Similarly, in the Australian state of Victoria, legal aid reform prioritised more serious crime and removed access to legal aid in all matters deemed unlikely to result in a custodial sentence. The decision was said to be justified 'on the basis that those facing the most severe form of punishment should be prioritised when there is competition for limited funds'. However, critics point out that in the light of incentives to plead guilty, and the serious consequences of doing so (including potential registration on the Sex Offenders Registry), there is a real risk of injustice due to induced guilty pleas being entered without appropriate advice: see Asher Flynn and others, *Access to Justice: A Comparative Analysis of Cuts to Legal Aid* (Report of the Monash Warwick Legal Aid Workshop, January 2015) at 5. Some self-represented defendants plead guilty despite having a defence: according to one interviewed prosecutor they 'are bullied by the clerks and bench into pleading guilty'. One magistrate said, 'they are told by the clerk if you plead guilty at the earliest opportunity the court will be more lenient than if you plead not guilty and are found guilty in the long run, so it's a bit of a game of poker in this respect'. In other instances, unrepresented defendants choose not to plead guilty when they may have, had they been properly advised; examples given occur where defendants do not understand the nature of party liability or conflate a legal defence with mitigating factors: see Transform Justice, *Justice Denied? The Experience of Unrepresented Defendants in the Criminal Courts* (April 2016) at 11–12.

encouraging early guilty pleas.[352] Pressures for lawyers to cut corners in prosecuting and in defending by reaching deals on pleas raise the risk of such errors.

Prosecution guidelines frankly acknowledge the considerable savings to the state in time and money through a guilty plea following what one guideline calls 'principled plea discussions and arrangements'.[353] Saved costs are one of the justifications for the sliding scale of discounts, according to when a plea is entered.[354] Defence counsel are encouraged

---

[352] *R v. Lawrence* [2013] EWCA Crim 1054, [2014] 1 WLR 106 where the defendant pleaded guilty to possessing a prohibited weapon but the weapon was not, in fact, prohibited.

[353] Crown Law, 'Solicitor-General's prosecution guidelines' (1 July 2013) at [18.1.2], available at: www.crownlaw.govt.nz (last accessed 11 November 2016). The guidelines indicate that prosecutors may take into account the cost of the proceeding in deciding whether it is in the public interest to continue with a prosecution even where there is sufficient evidence to do so (at [5.11]). The guidelines further provide (at [18.1]) that 'Principled plea discussions and arrangements have a significant value for the administration of the criminal justice system, including:

> Relieving victims or complainants of the burden of the trial process;
> Releasing the saved costs in Court and judicial time, prosecution costs, and legal aid resources to be better deployed in other areas of need;
> Providing a structured environment in which the defendant may accept any appropriate responsibility for his or her offending that may be reflected in any sentence imposed.'

[354] See the guidelines of the Sentencing Council, *Reduction in Sentence for a Guilty Plea Guideline: Consultation* (11 February 2016, London) at 7. While recognising the reluctance to provide a 'reward' for pleading guilty to those with little prospect of acquittal, the Sentencing Council

to focus on early resolution. Judges are brought into the process. The discretions they have to excuse delay in pleading and to give sentence indications mean that they operate some of the more important levers in obtaining disposal of cases through guilty pleas. This is the background in which some see the modern criminal justice system as characterised by 'mass production of guilty pleas' and a culture that measures the rate and timeliness of disposals as the principal marker of success.[355]

Guidelines for prosecutors direct them that charges must reflect the gravity of the offending. They cannot accept guilty pleas for convenience or in any case unless the court is able to impose a sentence that matches the seriousness of the offending.[356] These restrictions still leave room for considerable prosecutorial discretion, particularly in the assessment that a plea has been entered sufficiently promptly to attract

considered 'it is important to recognise that the guilty plea reduction is in place to provide an incentive . . . and not a reward. For it to work effectively it is important that it is a clear and unqualified incentive to the defendant.' The Sentencing Council also recognised that removal of a judge's ability to withhold reduction in cases of overwhelming evidence 'may be seen as an erosion of judicial discretion' but indicated this was outweighed by 'the Council's intention . . . to produce a guideline that promotes consistency and certainty': at 15. While the Sentencing Council emphasised that no one who is not guilty should be encouraged to plead guilty (at 13), the Bar Association has not been convinced that such discounts will not have that effect: see Criminal Bar Association of England and Wales, *CBA Response to the Sentencing Council Consultation on the Reduction in Sentence for a Guilty Plea Guidelines* (2016) at 2.

[355] See Andrew Sanders, Richard Young, and Mandy Burton, *Criminal Justice* (4th edn, Oxford University Press, 2010) at ch.8.

[356] Crown Prosecution Service, *The Code for Crown Prosecutors* (7th edn, January 2013) at [9.1]–[9.6].

higher discounts and in the attitude taken to minimum non-parole periods. In a number of jurisdictions, questions have been raised about the incentives placed on prosecutors to obtain early guilty pleas.[357] Such incentives may be set bureaucratically, by administrative targets, as has been suggested of the Crown Prosecution Service model.[358] Or prosecutors may in effect be incentivised to dispose of cases promptly by the funding model by which they are paid, as has been suggested to be the case with the bulk funding of Crown Solicitors in New Zealand,[359] which encourages minimising the time spent on cases. In 2012 a report on the Crown Prosecution Service in England and Wales expressed concerns about the basis on which pleas were accepted.[360] And there have been appellate criticisms of unaccountable reductions in charges to a level that does not reflect the gravity of the offending disclosed by the evidence.[361]

---

[357] See Andrew Ashworth and Jeremy Horder, *Principles of Criminal Law* (7th edn, Oxford University Press, 2013) at 80; Melvyn Green, 'Crown culture and wrongful convictions: a beginning' (2005) 25 *CR-ART* 262; *Barbaro* v. *The Queen* [2014] HCA 2, (2014) 253 CLR 58 at [31].

[358] Michael Zander, *The State of Justice* (The Hamlyn Lectures, Sweet & Maxwell, London, 2000) at 74.

[359] See Ronald Young, 'Has New Zealand's criminal justice system been compromised?' (Harkness Henry Lecture, University of Waikato, 7 September 2016).

[360] HM Crown Prosecution Service Inspectorate, *Follow up Report of the Thematic review of the Quality of Prosecution Advocacy and Case Presentation* (March 2012, London) at [3.8]. It found the need for improvement in respect of 'plea acceptance and basis of plea' and that compulsory training had not resulted in discernible improvement.

[361] See, for example, *R* v. *Goodings* [2012] EWCA Crim 2586. The Court allowed an appeal against sentence where the sentencing judge had sentenced on the basis of the higher charge justified by the evidence, but

While it is right to question whether the payment methods or administrative targets incentivise a push for guilty pleas, I wonder whether the incentives of pay or administrative agendas are as significant as other factors. If prosecutors are contributing to a culture of 'mass production of guilty pleas', the cause is more likely to be found in the relentless pressure of work, which may mark wider under-resourcing of the system or perhaps the setting of unrealistic targets in timeliness. There are a number of indicators of the work pressure under which prosecutors operate. They have been found in England and Wales to include reported failures by prosecutors to comply with disclosure requirements in a timely way and other indications of prosecutorial contribution to dely.[362] Some of the work

pointed out that the prosecution 'ought not to accept a plea of guilty to a charge which does not properly reflect the evidence or enable them properly to place before the court the facts which go to show the true gravity of the conduct': at [11]. In *Barbaro* v. *The Queen* [2014] HCA 2, (2014) 253 CLR 58, the High Court of Australia held that the prosecution should not be able to submit on appropriate sentencing ranges following a guilty plea, partly because prosecutors 'may have a view of the available sentencing range which gives undue weight to the avoidance of trial': at [31]. See also Mike McConville and Luke Marsh, *Criminal Judges: Legitimacy, Courts and State-Induced Guilty Pleas in Britain* (Edward Elgar, Cheltenham, 2014) at 138–9.

[362] The National Audit Office considers that delay in prosecution disclosure contributes significantly to the overall delays in the criminal justice system: Comptroller and Auditor General, *Efficiency in the Criminal Justice System* (National Audit Office, HC 852, 1 March 2016) at 22 (fig. 8). The Criminal Bar Association has suggested that the Crown Prosecution Service is failing to comply with obligations to provide sufficient evidence to defence counsel to enable timely advice as to pleas to be given to meet judicially set timetables. (The problem is said to be compounded by difficulties experienced by defence counsel in obtaining

pressure may be driven by the running down of resources for criminal justice more generally which makes it essential to keep courtrooms full and to move work out of the system and which transfers costs to participants who are not resourced to wear them.[363] Some pressures may be generated by the effort required by demonstration of compliance.

Charging decisions are difficult in cases of any factual complexity or where there are difficulties of proof. Initial charging decisions will often have to be reassessed as investigations are completed. Conscientiously undertaken, the work takes care and stamina and time. If the pressure of work does not provide the opportunity to reflect, the incentive to resolve cases will be strongest where they are most demanding of resources. These may often be cases in which there is heightened public interest in public determination of guilt. Whether a full discount

prison visits because of resourcing problems and shortage of facilities, a difficulty also reported in New Zealand.) See Criminal Bar Association of England and Wales, *CBA Response to the Sentencing Council Consultation on the Reduction in Sentence for a Guilty Plea Guidelines* (2016) at 1–2. There seems some substantiation of these complaints in the internal casework of the Crown Prosecution Service Inspectorate, which shows that in 2014–15 'the prosecution did not comply adequately with their initial disclosure obligations in 51% of sampled files' (as recorded in the National Audit Office report at 22 (fig. 8)).

[363] So, for example, prisons often have restricted facilities and resources to enable instructions to be taken effectively by defence counsel. Police are often inadequately resourced for preparation of witness statements, which often contain irrelevant and diffuse material, imposing further work on prosecutors and defence counsel.

for plea can be provided to a defendant or whether a non-parole period is imposed will depend very much on the attitude of the prosecutor, even if guidelines are tight. So there are plenty of temptations for quick resolutions or 'quick and casual' investigation or negotiation in a system where despatch of cases is valued over demonstration of correct outcomes.

There are comparable institutional and workload pressures on defence counsel. Whether or not it is designed to do so, reduction of fees for legal aid and fixed fees on a transaction model[364] means that the processing of a high volume of short, straightforward cases is generally more profitable for defence counsel than complex or fact-intensive work.[365] Guilty pleas at an early stage which do not entail

---

[364] The Access to Justice Act 1999 (UK) (described as 'unquestionably' the most major legal aid milestone since the introduction of civil legal aid in 1949 in Michael Zander, *The State of Justice* (The Hamlyn Lectures, Sweet & Maxwell, London, 2000) at 7) has been followed by other legislation, most recently the Legal Aid, Sentencing and Punishment of Offenders Act 2012 (UK). The legislation has heralded a transition towards fixed fees based around individual 'transactions' rather than holistic fee schemes. The rationale for these developments is cost-focused. In New Zealand, the Ministry of Justice, speaking of legal aid and its administration of the Public Defence Service, through which it 'ensures access to justice', says in its 2013–16 Statement of Intent '[o]ur focus is on ensuring these services remain sustainable and provide value for money': Ministry of Justice, *Statement of Intent 2013–2016* (2013, Wellington) at 13.

[365] The rationale for fixed fees is the concept of 'swings and roundabouts': swings are the more abundant, short, and straightforward cases, which are profitable for lawyers, whereas roundabouts are the infrequent, long, and complex cases. It has been commented of this model that, 'in

close consideration of evidence or law may pay best. There is room for concern that such payment structures may discourage full inquiry and consideration before a plea is entered, the time when legal advice is most needed to enable proper choice of the course of action available and in particular waiver of the right to silence.[366] In New Zealand, there has also been a shift of legal aid work to salaried public defenders employed by the Ministry of Justice. The Public Defence Service, which is intended to undertake 50 per cent of legal aid cases in courts in which it works, has led to the sort of questions about bureaucratic agendas that have been raised in England and Wales in relation to the Public Prosecution Service.[367]

a climate where fees are reduced to a low level for both types of work (and all types in between) one might argue that profitability no longer derives from the interplay of "swings and roundabouts", but merely from "swings"': see Tom Smith, 'Trust, choice and money: why the legal aid reform "u-turn" is essential for effective criminal defence' (2013) 11 *Crim L Rev* 906 at 911.

[366] See *Cadder* v. *HM Advocate* [2010] UKSC 43, [2010] 1 WLR 2601 at [45]–[55] per Lord Hope and at [93] Lord Rodger. I discussed waiver of the right to silence and the need for legal advice in the second Lecture.

[367] The 2013 Ministry of Justice objectives for the Public Defence Service is that '[t]he focus of the Public Defence Service over the next year will be to maximise efficiency by implementing new practice management software, developing and implementing nationally consistent business processes, and improving its reporting capability to monitor business performance': Ministry of Justice, *Statement of Intent 2013–2016* (2013, Wellington) at 13–14. There is research that suggests that cases managed by the Public Defence Service tend to result in greater use of guilty pleas, fewer changes of pleas, and fewer substantive hearings compared with private defence lawyers (see Sonia Ogier and Richard Tait, *Evaluation of the Public Defence Service Pilot* (Martin Jenkins, May 2008, Wellington)

In response to consultation on discounts for guilty pleas, in this country both the Law Society and Criminal Bar Association have pointed out that too often 'defendants and their representatives feel pressurised into entering a plea when there may be insufficient information' to enable solicitors to properly advise their clients.[368] There is a risk too that

at 2). It would not be fair to be critical about the Service on the basis of these results or to jump to the conclusion that the pleas are not appropriate. The Public Defence Service undertakes a high number of cases in the lowest categories, where guilty pleas are most likely. However, it is notable that the study of cases managed by the Public Defence Service concluded the differences in outcome 'cannot be explained by factors [like offence type, seriousness, and offender history] that are known to influence both pleas and case path' and were therefore seen as 'indicating that there is something particular about PDS cases that lead to these results'. There are moreover indications that some judges and court staff may feel able to make greater demands on the Public Defenders to accept fixtures for court efficiency reasons that require reassignment of counsel which may not be in the interests of clients on the basis that they are employed by a state agency.

[368] The Law Society of England and Wales commented '[t]he Society is aware of concerns, particularly amongst defence solicitors, that recent reforms of the criminal justice system, the reliance on case summaries and the expectation that a plea will be indicated at the first hearing in the magistrates' court or, in the case of an indictable offence, at a Plea and Trial Preparation Hearing, have created circumstances where defendants and their representatives feel pressurised into entering a plea when there may be insufficient information to enable solicitors, and other defence advocates, to properly discharge their professional duties to their clients'. Reasons for the lack of information include poorly drafted case and interview summaries and failure to properly identify key witnesses. Possible financial benefits from early resolution 'have to be viewed in the context of delays in the investigative process which are equally capable of causing concern to victims of crime and suspects‾

sentence indications may be given without sufficient information, particularly in relation to prosecution disclosure or
evidence bearing on mitigation.[369]

There are persistent suggestions that defence lawyers
are incentivised by legal aid payments to promote guilty
pleas.[370] A recent report has found that fixed fees have an

alike': Law Society of England and Wales, *Response to the Sentencing
Council Consultation on the Reduction in Sentence for a Guilty Plea
Guidelines* (May 2016) at 3–4. See also Criminal Bar Association of
England and Wales, *CBA Response to the Sentencing Council
Consultation on the Reduction in Sentence for a Guilty Plea Guidelines*
(2016) at 2: 'the stage at which the current proposals allow a defendant
full credit for a guilty plea lies before such evidence would have been
served. Few defendants wish to enter a guilty plea if they have an
alternative and thus there will clearly be pressure upon all defendants to
either plead guilty before they know if the state can prove the case
against them or lose credit for their plea.'

[369] In New Zealand, the Criminal Procedure Act 2011 provides that an
indication can be given if the court is 'satisfied that the information
available to it at that time is sufficient for that purpose': Criminal
Procedure Act 2011, s 61. The court must have an agreed statement of
facts; information on previous convictions; and a copy of any victim
impact statement. Drafters of the similar Victorian scheme were
concerned that if all relevant sentencing material were provided to the
judge, the process would no longer have efficiency benefits. This would
be particularly true if the defendant proceeded to trial anyway.
Commentators there have said there are evidential issues with the
scheme as constituted, in particular that full personal mitigation
information may not be available to the judge. See Asher Flynn,
'Sentence indications for indictable offences: increasing court efficiency
at the expense of justice? A response to the Victorian legislation' (2009)
42 *The Australian and New Zealand Journal of Criminology* 244 at 258–9.

[370] See Michael Zander, *The State of Justice* (The Hamlyn Lectures, Sweet &
Maxwell, London, 2000) at 69–72. In the Australian state of Victoria, the

impact on attendance of counsel at police stations.[371] As defence lawyers are less visible in police stations, there have been fears expressed in England and Wales of a re-emergence of 'police ploys' designed to discourage suspects from requesting legal advice.[372] One solicitor interviewed commented '[t]he new arrangements are giving the police a golden opportunity to go back to the sort of things they were doing in the 1980s, just before PACE'. That view appears to be borne out in New Zealand by recent cases heard by the Supreme Court where defendants who had received preliminary advice by telephone from lawyers available on a roster and who had been advised to say nothing until they had received full advice were persuaded or tricked into making damaging admissions.[373]

Legal Aid Commission recommended that an additional payment be provided for resolution at or before the first hearing to recognise the 'significant negotiations' necessary to achieve resolution: Victoria Legal Aid, 'Delivering high quality criminal trials – consultation and options paper' (January 2014) at 10. Lord Justice Leveson has endorsed this suggestion while expressing some concern that it could be seen as a financial incentive to recommend a guilty plea: Lord Justice Leveson, *Review of Efficiency in Criminal Proceedings* (January 2015) at [186]–[190].

[371] Research has shown that the introduction of fixed fees for legal advice offered at police stations, a payment which incorporates travel and waiting time, meant lawyers spent less time at the station waiting to see what charging decision was made. It was suggested that more junior staff were being sent: Vicky Kemp, 'Transforming legal aid: access to criminal defence services' (Legal Services Research Centre, September 2010) at 45 and n. 66.

[372] *Ibid.* at 45–6.

[373] In *R* v. *Perry* [2016] NZSC 102 the defendant was persuaded by a senior police officer that it would be better for him to make a statement

Some of the reforms to legal aid have been prompted by the view that criminal defence lawyers too often 'game' the system. In New Zealand, a critical report which preceded the latest reforms to legal aid suggested they took unnecessary steps or prolonged matters to hoist their fees.[374] While no doubt there was some justification for the adverse views about some lawyers, the conclusions are generally thought to have been exaggerated.[375] What has been particularly harmful in the indignation generated by these criticisms is the loss of insight into how onerous the work of defence counsel is. Questions of guilt may sometimes be clear. But very often they are not. That is especially true in cases of factual complexity or where guilt of the particular charge turns on what the defendant intended or knew or the capacity in which he or she was involved in group offending.

There are indications that defence counsel, like prosecutors, are under great pressure in their work. In England, the agencies responsible for legal aid have reported concerns about non-compliance with proper standards of performance

promptly if he thought he was not implicated in the death under investigation. In *R* v. *Kumar* [2015] NZSC 124, [2016] 1 NZLR 204 undercover officers were placed in the defendant's cell and elicited the admissions by playing the part of other arrested persons. Because under New Zealand legislation (s 30 of the Evidence Act 2006) the courts will exclude incriminating statements improperly obtained only if exclusion is proportionate to the impropriety, it may seem to the police to be worth pushing matters in this way.

[374] Legal Aid Review, *Transforming the Legal Aid System: Final Report and Recommendations* (Ministry of Justice, November 2009) at viii.

[375] See Kim Economides, 'Reforming legal aid' [2010] *NZLJ* 5.

by legal aid lawyers.[376] Practitioners, certainly in my jurisdiction, say themselves that the work is relentless and that space to prepare or think is almost impossible to fit in around the remorseless scheduling that is required by courts' administration.

The public interest in proper conviction as well as the interest of the individual suggest that we should not be casual about allowing time for legal advisers to understand the facts of the case and be in a position to give proper advice which the defendant has time to consider. Rush to plea is not a goal we should be pursuing. And it should not be something that case management exacerbates.

---

[376] A 1997 report by the Legal Aid Board indicated that police station advisers had high levels of non-compliance with the performance standards laid down by the Law Society; see *Legal Aid Board Annual Report* (1997–98) at [5.12], as cited in Michael Zander, *The State of Justice* (The Hamlyn Lectures, Sweet & Maxwell, London, 2000) at 69. Research in Scotland from 2006 indicated that changes in remuneration can alter defence lawyers' case management decisions. Reform there implemented fixed fees, which were designed to encourage early guilty pleas but which would be paid only if there was an initial 'not guilty' plea. Lawyers were financially disadvantaged by disposing of cases quickly. Following review, the scheme was amended in a manner to encourage defence lawyers to deal with cases by way of a guilty plea at the earliest opportunity, a change that had the desired effect of increasing the number of early guilty pleas. The Scottish study also contained suggestions from interviewed solicitors that the quality of decisions was affected and that there was a greater risk of miscarriage of justice, although it did not contain empirical data on that issue: see Vicky Kemp, 'Transforming legal aid: access to criminal defence services' (Legal Services Research Centre, September 2010) at 112–14.

Judges have been drawn into the promotion of guilty pleas. New Zealand now has an elaborate system for sentence indications by judges, established by legislation and available before plea.[377] The judge can determine whether or not to give a sentence indication and, if so, the type of indication to be given.[378] Increasingly, judges have been prepared to indicate the sentence considered appropriate before the defendant pleads, rather than giving a range or indication that it will be custodial or non-custodial. There is general acknowledgement that the willingness to give such indications has led to an increase in guilty pleas.[379] It has to be acknowledged that in some courts and among some judges the preparedness to give sentence indications was evident before the legislation permitted it and was seen as an effective tool of case management. Other jurisdictions have been more cautious about

---

[377] Before enactment of legislation in 2011, such indications had often been given in the District Court as part of a judicial initiative for case management but were rarely given in the High Court.

[378] Criminal Procedure Act 2011, ss 60–5. For the policy behind the Act and critique of sentencing indications, see New Zealand Law Commission, *Pre-Trial Processes: Justice Through Efficiency* (NZLC R89, 2005) at [304]–[340].

[379] See for example Geoffrey Venning (Chief High Court Judge), *Report from the High Court 2015 – the Year in Review* (17 May 2016) at 6. The New Zealand Law Society reported that the number of sentence indications requested has increased steadily since the relevant Act came into force in March 2012. It was reported that 82 per cent of sentence indication applications are granted by the courts, 14 per cent are withdrawn or discontinued by the defendant, and 4 per cent are rejected: New Zealand Law Society, 'A quarter of sentencing indication applications are falling through' (26 February 2015), available at: www.lawsociety.org.nz (last accessed 11 November 2016).

sentence indications, permitting indications of maximums only or whether a custodial sentence is in prospect. So, in England and Wales, under appellate guidance and practice directions, judges in the Crown Court may indicate a maximum sentence to be imposed if a guilty plea is made at the stage of the indication.[380] In Victoria, judges may indicate whether a custodial or non-custodial sentence would be imposed.[381]

Obtaining pleas through sentence indications is now, however, widely seen as an important end of case management. It is difficult to get a handle on whether judges are consciously or unconsciously attempting to obtain pleas by offering discounts that provide incentives. I have been surprised to hear senior judges speak of success in obtaining pleas on sentence indications. And it is troubling to hear senior practitioners say that at pre-trial review hearings it is not unknown for judges to interrogate defendants directly, even defendants who are represented, about the defence or the conduct of the case. Some judges are said to give sentence indications without invitation in an apparent effort to move a case to resolution. It is also worrying to hear reports that counsel both for the defence and for the Crown sometimes feel under pressure from the judge when seeking necessary

---

[380] Guidance was established by the Court of Appeal in R v. Goodyear [2005] EWCA Crim 888, [2005] 1 WLR 2532 and is set out in the Criminal Practice Directions [2015] EWCA Crim 1567. For indications in the magistrates' court as to whether a sentence will be custodial, amendments were introduced by sch. 3 of the Criminal Justice Act 2003, which amended the Magistrates' Courts Act 1980.

[381] Under the Criminal Procedure Act 2009 (Vic), ss 207–9.

adjournments or when seeking further disclosure on the basis that there is little point because the defendant knows what he has done. It is difficult to know whether these reports give an accurate picture of what is happening. They are, however, commonly heard. If they indicate a shift in culture in which judges assume responsibility for managing cases to achieve prompt guilty pleas, they represent a move away from the idea of the detached judge.

Judges have always attempted to move cases along and prevent waste of everyone's time. In dealing with procedural directions for trial, judges have not been so detached as to be receptive to applications which would prolong or proliferate issues for trial or cause more work for the system. That is illustrated by the relatively austere approach taken to severance[382] and it is shown in judicial statements supportive

---

[382] So, for example, in England and Wales, Australia, and New Zealand, judges have been reluctant to order separate trials for defendants, requiring something overwhelming before doing so and relying on jury directions to meet fairness problems even though such directions are of a complexity that is not usually countenanced. Glanville Williams has commented on the 'simple faith that the jury are able to follow [the] direction' to disregard evidence in relation to other accused, which he says is 'curiously inconsistent with the effort made by other rules of law to prevent the jury coming to know of evidence that may be misleading': Glanville Williams, *The Proof of Guilt: A Study of the English Criminal Trial* (The Hamlyn Lectures, Stevens & Sons, London, 1955) at 186. In Canada, by contrast, the approach seems a more open-minded assessment of trial fairness: see *R* v. *Last* 2009 SCC 45, [2009] 3 SCR 146 at [16]–[18]. By way of example, see in New Zealand *Churchis* v. *R* [2014] NZCA 281, (2014) 27 CRNZ 257; and *R* v. *Smith* [2008] NZCA 266 at [14]; in England and Wales *R* v. *Lake* (1977) 64 Cr App R 172 (CA); and *R* v.

of defence disclosure to avoid 'ambush by the defence'[383] (an attitude not followed in Canada where defence disclosure is seen to infringe the right to silence).[384] There are, too, plenty of examples of judges giving juries steers to conviction rather than staying above the fray. But that has not been the ideal or what has been professed. And achievement of disposals through sentence indications takes matters to a new level. Has there been removal of some judicial inhibitions in criminal justice? And does it pose risks for some of the values we have treated as fundamental to criminal justice?

I do not have any clear answer but I do have a cautionary tale. It is one about appellate case management rather than case management of trials. And I should first say something about appellate responsibility. Professor Glanville Williams thought that appellate supervision in common law jurisdictions had been greatly restricted by what he regarded as the 'exaggerated deference accorded to the jury'.[385] I have

---

Hayter [2005] UKHL 6, [2005] 1 WLR 605; and in Australia *Webb* v. *The Queen* (1994) 181 CLR 41.

[383] *R* v. *Rochford* [2010] EWCA Crim 1928, [2011] 1 WLR 534 at [10]; see also *R* v. *Penner* [2010] EWCA Crim 1155; and *R* v. *Gleeson* [2003] EWCA Crim 2160, [2004] 1 Cr App R 406 at 416. In South Australia, a current proposal would greatly extend the disclosure required beyond that required in England and Wales under s 6A of the Criminal Procedure and Investigation Act 1996 (UK): see Attorney-General's Department, *Transforming Criminal Justice Consultation Paper: Efficient Progression and Resolution of Major Indictable Matters* (March 2015).

[384] *R* v. *P (MB)* [1994] 1 SCR 555 at 578 per Lamer CJ; see also *R* v. *Stinchcombe* [1991] 3 SCR 326 at 333.

[385] Glanville Williams, *The Proof of Guilt: A Study of the English Criminal Trial* (The Hamlyn Lectures, Stevens & Sons, London, 1955) at 259.

more time for the jury, but I agree that the excuse provided by
the jury and its 'constitutional position' as trier of fact has
tended to inhibit appellate responsibility and make it difficult
for appeals to be brought against jury verdicts. That inhibited
approach did not I think ever properly accord with the terms
of the appeal ground that the verdict was against the weight of
the evidence.[386] And I do not think it can properly be maintained today, at least in New Zealand where a right of appeal is
recognised as a human right[387] and no leave requirement
applies.[388]

Now that the jury is not required in all criminal cases
of any seriousness and there is increasing recourse to judge-
alone trials, there seems little basis on which to draw
a distinction in the scope of the right of appeal according to
whether the trier of fact is judge or jury. It is true that the
provision of reasons will make it easier to spot an error in
the verdict of a judge than in the verdict of a jury. But where

---

[386] Under 385(1) of the Crimes Act 1961, the appeal had to be allowed if the
jury's verdict was 'unreasonable or cannot be supported having regard
to the evidence'. This language was altered by s 232(2) of the Criminal
Procedure Act 2011. An appeal in a jury trial must be allowed if 'having
regard to the evidence, the jury's verdict was unreasonable'. Under both
enactments, an appeal would also be allowed if for any reason there was
a miscarriage of justice. In the important decision of the High Court of
Australia in *Weiss* v. *R* [2005] HCA 81, (2005) 224 CLR 300, the High
Court was clear that it was not useful to speak of the accused having
a 'right' to the verdict of the jury once an appellate court may set aside
a jury's verdict on the ground that it is unreasonable or cannot be
supported having regard to the evidence: see at [28]–[30]. The task for
the court is not materially different from other appellate tasks: at [39].
[387] New Zealand Bill of Rights Act 1990, s 25(h).
[388] Criminal Procedure Act 2011, s 213(2).

the question for the appellate court is whether the proof of guilt was sufficient, there is no help but to review the evidence to the extent at least that the argument on appeal takes you there. And then, as has now at last been established in the UK and in Australia and New Zealand, the appellate court itself must be satisfied of guilt before a conviction can be upheld and does not have to imagine how a jury might have dealt with particular evidence or have reasoned.[389]

It has to be said that the prospect of reviewing the evidence where the appeal requires it is not always welcome to busy intermediate courts of appeal. But experiences with miscarriages of justice indicate why second looks are absolutely necessary and why they need to be open-minded.

The cautionary tale I want to tell concerns the New Zealand Court of Appeal.[390] At the end of the 1980s, overwhelmed with criminal appeals and the number of unrepresented appellants, the Court set up a system for expediting consideration of legal aid and appeals. At that time, legal aid was granted by the registrar of the court, with a right of review by a judge of the Court. The Court took the view that the process of legal aid and determination of the substantive

---

[389] *R* v. *Pendleton* [2001] UKHL 66, [2002] 1 WLR 72. See also Lord Kerr, '*Miscarriage of justice – when should an appellate court quash conviction?*' (16 December 2013, JUSTICE Scotland International Human Rights Day Lecture, Edinburgh). In Australia, see *Weiss* v. *R* [2005] HCA 81, (2005) 224 CLR 300; and in New Zealand, see *R* v. *Matenga* [2009] NZSC 18, [2009] 3 NZLR 145 at [31]; *Lundy* v. *R* [2013] UKPC 28, [2014] 2 NZLR 273 at [144]–[150].

[390] *Taito* v. *R* [2003] UKPC 15, [2003] 3 NZLR 577. This summary is taken from that provided by Lord Steyn in delivering the advice of the Board: at [1]–[3] and [8].

appeal would be expedited by having the initial legal aid decision taken by a panel of three judges of the Court. Because the three judges had jurisdiction to determine the substantive appeal, the Court considered that the determination by three judges that the case was unworthy of a grant of legal aid could safely be treated as a dismissal of the appeal. The Court therefore put in place a system which fulfilled the steps required by the legislation, but which was a shortcut. Three judges of the Court considered the question of legal aid on the papers. They directed the registrar to dismiss the applications if the appeal was thought to have no merit. Review of the legal aid determination (as was provided for by legislation if sought) was then dismissed by a single judge without hearing or reasons. The appeals in which legal aid had been declined were then listed for what the Court called 'ex parte dismissal'. The appellants were not present. Although the appellants had been told they had the right to lodge written submissions, very few did. If no submissions were lodged by unrepresented appellants, the Court dismissed the appeals without further examination of the merits by the judges listed for the ex parte dismissals and without reasons. In the rare cases where written submissions were received, the appeals were dismissed with brief reasons written up by one of the judges on the legal aid panel or by the judge who had reviewed the legal aid decision. The view taken by the Court in adopting this streamlined procedure was that if three members of the Court had concluded that the case did not merit legal aid, it had no realistic prospect of success.

In 2000, the Privy Council said of this procedure that it was 'extra-legal'.[391] The requirements of the Crimes Act 1961 that the judgment be in accordance with the opinion of the judges present at its delivery was incapable of fulfilment. The *ex parte* decisions were said by the Privy Council to be 'purely formalistic or mechanical acts involving no exercise of judicial judgment'. The earlier legal aid decisions could not be treated as the substantive judgment of the court because they were not taken after hearing. Nor did the judges ever meet to discuss the cases. The procedure was in breach of the Crimes Act and the Bill of Rights Act. The Board concluded that although the adoption of the procedure had been 'well intentioned' and a response to the need to find a practical and just way to dispose of unmeritorious appeals, the '[d]ecisions that the appeals were in truth unmeritorious could only be made after observance of procedural due process' and the system 'failed this basic test'. Worse still, the procedure had discriminated between those with the means to obtain legal representation and those without the means. It did not provide the record of the case to the unrepresented appellants, even where it was referred to in the judgment of the Court of Appeal. The record was, however, provided to the counsel of represented litigants.

The case was a salutary correction. The judges of the Court of Appeal, the very best we have had, took their eyes off the ball because they were managing their workload to achieve effective and efficient outcomes. The aftermath was that it was necessary to give public notice that all appeals

[391] At [13]–[20].

dismissed under the process over the 12-year period it was in place could be heard again. Many appellants had served out their sentences and did not seek a hearing. It is not known how many did. But two murder convictions were quashed as a result of the new hearings.[392]

Conclusion

Miss Hamlyn had two objects in her imaginative bequest. She hoped that the Lectures she endowed would demonstrate the privileges which in law and custom we have inherited. The second object was to illuminate the responsibilities that attach to those privileges. I happen to think that our system of criminal justice is something to be proud of, as I am sure Miss Hamlyn believed it to be. I also believe she was right to think that the privileges of the system can only be maintained if it is understood and valued by everyone. The challenge in our time for criminal justice is one of legitimacy.

If it is to be legitimate, the great coercive power of the state must be applied in a manner that is 'uniform, equal, and predictable'.[393] It must proceed, as Roscoe Pound thought, 'from reason and upon understood grounds rather than from caprice or impulse or without full and fair hearing of all affected and understanding of the facts on which official

---

[392] *R* v. *Sadaraka* CA274/03, 27 May 2004; *Timoti* v. *R* [2005] NZSC 37, [2006] 1 NZLR 323, which allowed an appeal from *R* v. *Timoti* [2005] 1 NZLR 466 (CA).

[393] Roscoe Pound, *The Development of Constitutional Guarantees of Liberty* (Yale University Press, New Haven, 1957) at 1.

action is taken'.[394] Such process may not be speedy and it is not likely to be cheap. I do not expect criminal justice ever was speedy or cheap. Its careful observance is, however, best policy for a 'law-state'.[395] The forms and delays which attend legal process 'are necessary to guard the person and the property of the citizen', as Edward Gibbon acknowledged at the end of the eighteenth century.[396] 'The history of liberty has largely been the history of observance of procedural safeguards', as Frankfurter J thought in the middle of the twentieth century.[397] I do not know why we would think that such insights are not valid today.

In 1840, Thomas Babbington Macaulay concluded an article in the *Edinburgh Review* with a startling image of a traveller from New Zealand in some distant future 'tak[ing] his stand on a broken arch of London Bridge to sketch the ruins of St Paul's'.[398] I have wondered in putting together this Lecture whether it may seem that this traveller from New Zealand is attempting a sketch of the ruins of the criminal justice system we have shared since the year in which Macaulay wrote. I hope it does not seem so. I am not so

---

[394] At 1.

[395] See Neil MacCormick, 'Institutional normative order: a conception of law' (1997) 82 *Cornell L Rev* 1051.

[396] Edward Gibbon, *The History of the Decline and Fall of the Roman Empire* (Robinson, London, 1830) at 779.

[397] *McNabb v. United States* 318 US 332 (1943) at 347.

[398] T.B. Macaulay, 'Review of Leopold von Ranke: the ecclesiastical and political history of the popes during the sixteenth and seventeenth centuries' (1840) 72 *Edinburgh Review* 227 at 258.

pessimistic. But it is necessary to acknowledge that the system is under stress.

The deliberation, calmness, and care in public and even-handed proof of guilt of crime come at a cost that our societies seem less willing to pay as the price of civilisation and good government than in the past. 'Cool impartial justice' seems less valued. There is impatience with an accusatory method of proof conducted on behalf of the state and tested by the defence before a judge who comes to the case as a judge only. These attitudes may be corrosive.

The determination of guilt of those accused of criminal offences was said by Mary Gaudron of the High Court of Australia to be 'the most important of all judicial functions'.[399] It was essential, she thought, that such proceedings be conducted 'according to rules of general application' because that feature distinguished between 'palm tree justice and equal justice'. Without demonstration of equal justice the integrity of the courts and public confidence in the legal system could not be maintained.

Today, too much criminal justice is conducted out of the public gaze and with outcomes that are not sufficiently explained and which may be discriminatory in effect. Those involved in the system are under pressures that risk error. This is an area where we cannot afford to be indifferent to error without compromising the legitimacy of the legal order. There is particular risk to legitimacy if more punitive

---

[399] *Kable* v. *Director of Public Prosecutions for the State of New South Wales (NSW)* (1996) 189 CLR 51 at 107.

outcomes fall disproportionately on distinct populations. If it is cost pressures that are leading to justice out of public sight and at the discretion of law enforcement officers, then the question posed by Dame Hazel Genn of civil justice is even more urgent in the case of criminal justice: 'How much justice can we afford to forego?'[400]

[400] Hazel Genn, *Judging Civil Justice* (The Hamlyn Lectures, Cambridge University Press, 2010) at 15.